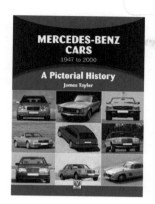

MERCEDES-BENZ CARS
1947 to 2000

A Pictorial History

James Taylor

A Pictorial History - more titles in this series
Austin Cars 1948 to 1990 (Rowe)
Citroën Cars 1934 to 1986 (Parish)
Ford Cars – Ford UK cars 1945-1995 (Rowe)
Jaguar Cars 1946 to 2008 (Thorley)
Morris Cars 1948 to 1984 (Newell)
Riley & Wolseley Cars 1948 to 1975 (Rowe)
Rootes Cars of the 50s, 60s & 70s – Hillman, Humber, Singer, Sunbeam & Talbot (Rowe)
Rover Cars 1945 to 2005 (Taylor)
Triumph & Standard Cars 1945 to 1984 (Warrington)
Vauxhall Cars 1945 to 1995 (Alder)
Volvo Cars 1945 to 1985 (Alder)

Veloce's Essential Buyer's Guides
Mercedes-Benz 190: all 190 models (W201 series) 1982 to 1993 (Parish)
Mercedes-Benz 280-560SL & SLC (Bass)
Mercedes-Benz G-Wagen (Greene)
Mercedes-Benz Pagoda 230SL, 250SL & 280SL roadsters & coupés (Bass)
Mercedes-Benz S-Class W126 Series (Zoporowski)
Mercedes-Benz S-Class Second Generation W116 Series (Parish)
Mercedes-Benz SL R129-series 1989 to 2001 (Parish)
Mercedes-Benz SLK (Bass)
Mercedes-Benz W123 (Parish)
Mercedes-Benz W124 – All models 1984-1997 (Zoporowski)

Other Mercedes-Benz titles
Max Hoffman – Million Dollar Middleman (Kornblatt)
Mercedes-Benz SL – W113-series 1963-1971 (Long)
Mercedes-Benz SL & SLC – 107-series 1971-1989 (Long)
Mercedes-Benz SLK – R170 series 1996-2004 (Long)
Mercedes-Benz SLK – R171 series 2004-2011 (Long)
Mercedes-Benz W123-series – All models 1976 to 1986 (Long)
Mercedes-Benz W124 series – 1984-1997 (Long)
Mercedes G-Wagen (Long)
Return to Glory! The Mercedes-Benz 300 SL Racing Car (Ackerson)
Two Summers – The Mercedes-Benz W196R Racing Car (Ackerson)

www.veloce.co.uk

First published in 2024 by Veloce, an imprint of David and Charles Limited. Tel +44 (0)1305 260068 / e-mail info@veloce.co.uk / web www.veloce.co.uk.
ISBN: 978-1-845843-31-1; UPC: 6-36847-04331-5 © 2024 James Taylor and David and Charles. All rights reserved. With the exception of quoting brief passages for the
purpose of review, no part of this publication may be recorded, reproduced or transmitted by any means, including photocopying, without the written permission of David
and Charles Limited.
Throughout this book logos, model names and designations, etc, have been used for the purposes of identification, illustration and decoration. Such names are the
property of the trademark holder as this is not an official publication. Readers with ideas for automotive books, or books on other transport or related hobby subjects, are
invited to write to the editorial director of Veloce at the above address. British Library Cataloguing in Publication Data – A catalogue record for this book is available from
the British Library. Design and production by Veloce. Printed in the UK by TJ Books.

MERCEDES-BENZ CARS

1947 to 2000

A Pictorial History

James Taylor

Veloce

CONTENTS

Introduction

The success story of Mercedes-Benz cars in the half-century following the Second World War is a remarkable one. The company's factories had been bombed into ruins to hinder its contribution to the German war machine, and when peace came it took a considerable time before the company returned to its former prominence within the German car industry.

Although Mercedes' first postwar cars were revived prewar designs, a dogged determination to succeed resulted in some remarkably modern machinery in the early years of the 1950s. Expansion into export markets, especially the USA, helped to bring in the necessary funds, and by the middle of the 1950s Mercedes was once again a force to be reckoned with, not just in West Germany (the country was then still divided into two) but globally.

This book details the passenger car model ranges that were built between 1947 and 2000 and, inevitably, strays into the early years of the 21st century, because existing model-ranges did not end production neatly at the turn of the millennium. By then, Mercedes had embarked on a new model policy that gave greater consideration to marketing than in earlier years, when its engineers had been the dominant and severely rational force within the company.

For readers new to the Mercedes range, a few notes will be in order. Model names were given a code number, which in the early years was preceded by a W (for Wagen, or car). In later years, as model ranges expanded, the W might be replaced by C (coupé or cabriolet), R (roadster), S (estate) or A (convertible). Engine type codes were preceded by an M (for motor) or OM (ölmotor or diesel engine).

Performance figures and dimensions are shown in the units favoured in Germany in order to maintain some consistency, so engine outputs are in PS (Pferdestärke, horsepower) and Nm (Newton-metres, for torque), speeds in km/h (kilometres per hour), and dimensions in metric units. However, fuel consumption is shown in mpg (miles per gallon) for the benefit of UK and US readers for whom litres per 100 kilometres is generally a step too far. (Note, though, that US gallons are smaller than the imperial measurements used in the UK and in this book!)

A very large percentage of the photographs used in these pages have come from Daimler-Benz AG, the parent company of Mercedes-Benz, and I am very grateful to the press and museum staff who have provided these over the 40-odd years that have marked my serious interest in the cars. I am also very grateful indeed to those generous souls who have made their work available for reproduction through Wikimedia Commons, and who are credited individually alongside the relevant photographs. A small number of pictures (usually the less crisp ones, sadly) are my own.

There are very many books about Mercedes cars in print, and not a few of them have my own name on the cover. This present title can only give an outline of the story, which would need several very large volumes to cover thoroughly. For readers who want to take their interest further, I can only encourage a search on the internet (or, in the old-fashioned way, at a library) to find further enlightenment.

James Taylor
Oxfordshire, 2024

The 170 ranges, 1947-1955

Car makers on both sides of the conflict in the Second World War had been diverted to production for the war effort and had no option but to re-introduce their prewar models when peace returned in 1945. For Mercedes, car production was still two years away. After some heroic efforts to clear the rubble from its bomb-damaged factories and get production running again, the company restarted with the chassis of its prewar 170V model in June 1946, which it supplied to various concerns for bodying as a van, a pick-up, or an ambulance to meet the areas of greatest need.

Before car production restarted, Mercedes turned out light commercials on the saloon chassis.

Saloons followed in May 1947 and were very similar indeed to the prewar W136 models. They were four-door types with no external access to the boot, flowing wings linked by vestigial running-boards, and the spare wheel exposed on the tail. Underneath was a cruciform backbone chassis, along with independent front suspension, and the trusty 1697cc side-valve four-cylinder engine driving through an all-synchromesh four-speed gearbox.

The 170V followed on from the prewar saloon, and the diesel 170D was added. By the time of this one, an opening boot lid was standard.

Before the war, Mercedes had been a pioneer of diesel power for cars, and the difficult economic circumstances of the late 1940s prompted a further look at this method of propulsion. At the Hanover Fair in May 1949, the company introduced the 170D model – basically a 170V with a new diesel engine that gave 40mpg, nearly twice the economy of the petrol type. In fact, the engine shared the dimensions of its petrol sibling, but now had pushrod-operated overhead valves and an indirect-injection cylinder head.

The 170 range was gradually developed. This is a 170Va or 170Da, built between 1950 and 1952.

The range was expanded upwards at the same time in 1949. The 170S introduced higher equipment levels and a slightly modernised design related to the prewar 230 six-cylinder and offering more interior room. A big-bore 1767cc engine with light-alloy cylinder head, and suspension changes that included rubber bushes all round and a redesigned layout at the front, added refinements not visible to the eye. More important was that alongside this saloon came a pair of new cabriolet derivatives, which reflected both the increasing strength of the German economy

The 170S brought a more modern body style. This is a 170S-D models from 1953.

Also based on the 170S was this special police troop carrier model.

Some bare chassis were supplied to specialist coachbuilders. This estate model was built by Hägele of Mössingen.

and Mercedes' optimism for the future. These are discussed in more detail in Chapter 5.

The early 1950s saw more changes. Six-cylinder 220S models took over from the 170S cabriolets and the saloons were revised to become W191 models. There were 170S (strictly 170Sb) and 170DS types, and these carried the range through alongside the less expensive 170V and 170D models until the brand-new Ponton types were introduced in autumn 1953. Even then, the old 170 range was not finished: improved 170S-V and 170S-D models, both based on the older W136 design despite the slightly misleading names, catered for the lower end of the market until 1955. More than 153,000 of all the postwar 170 models had been built by the time production ended.

MODELS: 170V, 170D (1947-1953); 170S (1949-1953); 170DS (1952-1953); 170S-V, 170S-D (1953-1955).
ENGINES: 1697cc M136 petrol four with 38PS or (from 1950) 45PS; 1697cc OM636 diesel four with 38PS or (from 1950) 40 PS;

1767cc petrol four with 52PS or (from 1953) 45PS; 1767cc diesel four with 40 PS.
GEARBOX: Four-speed all-synchromesh manual.
SUSPENSION, STEERING & BRAKES: Front suspension with twin wishbones and transverse leaf springs (170V & 170D) or coil springs and anti-roll bar (all later models). Rear suspension with swing axles and coil springs. Worm steering. Drum brakes on all four wheels.
DIMENSIONS: Length: 4507mm (170V & 170D); 4455mm (all later models). **Width:** 1580mm (170V & 170D); 1684mm (all later models). **Height:** 1610mm. **Wheelbase:** 2845mm. **Track:** 1310mm (front), 1296mm (rear), 1342mm 170Va & Da; 1360mm 170Vb & Db; 1315mm (front), 1420mm (rear) 170S; 1315mm (front), 1435mm (rear) 170Sb, 170DS, 170S-V & 170S-D.
PERFORMANCE & FUEL CONSUMPTION:
170V: 67mph, 21mpg, 0-100km/h in 34.0 sec;
170D: 62mph, 31mpg, 0-100km/h in 50 sec;
170S: 76mph, 19mpg, 0-100km/h in 32 sec;
170DS: 65mph, 27mpg, 0-100km/h in 56 sec;
170S-V: 71mph, 20mpg, 0-100km/h in 39 sec;
170S-D: 65mph, 27mpg, 0-100km/h in 56 sec.
PRODUCTION TOTALS: 170V: 47,082 (including bare chassis); vans, pick-ups, Police specials, ambulances, etc: 2285; 170D: 33,307 (including bare chassis and Police specials); vans 515; 170S: 28,764, plus 56 bare chassis; 170Sb: 8080 plus 14 bare chassis; 170DS: 12,857 plus 128 bare chassis; 170S-V: 3002 plus 120 bare chassis; 170S-D: 11,800 plus 3087 bare chassis.

The 220, 1951-1954

Mercedes had to proceed in small steps as the company regained its stride after the Second World War. Incremental changes gradually updated the 170 range, but from an early stage the aim was to be ready with more expensive six-cylinder models as soon as the time was right. There were to be two six-cylinder engines: one for the big limousine flagship range that became the 300, and the other with a smaller capacity for a model more closely related to the 170S.

That less expensive model was announced as the 220 at the Frankfurt Motor Show in

The six-cylinder 220 used the heavier body style and was easily identified by chrome strakes on the front wing crowns.

April 1951 alongside the 170 range. Its works designation was W187. Visually, it was very similar to the 170S but redesigned front wings with the headlamps in their leading edges gave it a distinctive appearance. There were saloon models and more expensive cabriolet and coupé types, which are discussed in Chapter 5. Saloons could be ordered with a folding fabric sunroof.

The big news of course was the six-cylinder engine, a 2195cc oversquare OHC design with 80PS that was matched to carefully chosen gearing, giving both good acceleration and stress-free high-speed Autobahn cruising. Typical of the times, perhaps, was the choice of a column-mounted gear selector, which reflected the American influence. It was not a short-lived fad, however, and column selectors would remain available on Mercedes for many more years.

The chassis was once again Mercedes' favoured oval-section cruciform backbone type, while the all-round independent suspension was similar to that of the 170S and depended on coil springs, with an anti-roll bar at the front. A total of 41 W187 220 models were bodied as police personnel carriers, and just two received custom coachwork (by Drews in Essen and Wendler in Reutlingen) while a further 45 bare chassis were variously bodied as vans, ambulances, and police radio cars, which had an estate-like configuration.

Sales were always steady rather than spectacular, and peaked as early as 1952. There were no exports to the USA, and the cars did not reach the UK until 1954, where Purchase Tax made them so expensive that sales were tiny. Mercedes ended production that year, by which time the far more modern 220 Ponton was ready as a replacement.

MODELS: 220 saloon.
ENGINE: 2195cc M180 petrol six with 80PS.
GEARBOX: Four-speed all-synchromesh manual.
SUSPENSION, STEERING & BRAKES: Front suspension with twin wishbones, coil springs and anti-roll bar. Rear suspension with swing axles and double coil springs. Worm steering. Drum brakes on all four wheels.
DIMENSIONS: Length: 4507mm. **Width:**

The 220 also had an enclosed boot, like the 170S. (Lothar Spurzem, CC by SA 2.0)

There were special police versions of the 220, too, this one being a four-door Tourer.

1685mm. **Height:** 1610mm. **Wheelbase:** 2845mm. **Track:** 1315mm (front), 1485mm (rear).
PERFORMANCE & FUEL CONSUMPTION: 220 87mph, 17mpg, 0-100km/h in 21.0 sec.
PRODUCTION TOTAL: 16,154, including Police specials and bare chassis.

The Ponton models, 1953-1962

The Ponton range was so-called because a German journalist wrote that its monocoque construction reminded him of a pontoon bridge (Ponton is the German for pontoon). This kind of self-supporting construction, which dispensed with a separate chassis, was not new in itself but it was new to Mercedes when its new saloon range was introduced in 1953.

Internally, the first Pontons were W120 types. The Mercedes plan was to create as wide a range of cars as possible from the basic design, and in that aim it certainly succeeded. That basic design was a four-door saloon with full-width styling that appeared modern when new, and the initial release was of the 180 model with an updated version of the 170S petrol engine. A diesel 180D equivalent followed a year later, and these two models would form the backbone of the range until its demise in 1962. They also became its best-sellers, and the 180D in particular established the medium-sized Mercedes as a taxi-drivers' favourite across the globe.

There were of course progressive improvements as engine power was increased, but the inevitable six-cylinder derivative arrived to top the range in 1954. This had a longer nose to accommodate the longer engine, which resulted in very pleasing proportions.

The engine was a further development of the earlier 220S type, but for now the six-cylinder Ponton saloon was simply called a 220. Later it became known as a 220a internally, and it always had its own designation of W180.

The next major changes came in 1956. The 180 was supplemented by a 190 with enlarged four-cylinder petrol engine and W121 designation. The six-cylinder range was now split into two as a more powerful twin-carburettor 220S replaced the 220 and a less expensive 219 model was created by putting the 220's engine into a short-nose bodyshell, a combination that earned the unique designation of W105. While the original four-speed gearbox was always standard, an automatic clutch called the Hydrak was made optional on six-cylinder cars in 1957, but it was never very popular and few have survived.

The 190 was joined by a 190D with enlarged diesel engine in 1958 and was then upgraded in 1959 as a 190b. Meanwhile, in 1958 the new top model 220SE was introduced, with an injected version of the six-cylinder engine and higher performance.

Meanwhile, the range had expanded in other ways. First came part-built four-cylinder models that were shipped to conversion specialists to become pick-ups, vans, ambulances, estates, hearses and other 'specials'. The basic Ponton floorpan was shortened to become the basis of the 190SL sports car in 1954 (and that is discussed in Chapter 4). Then there were special two-door prestige derivatives of the six-cylinder range from 1956 (and these are discussed in Chapter 5).

The result of all this was that the Ponton range was produced in far larger quantities than any of its predecessors. The Mercedes determination to amortise high development costs with large sales volumes paid off handsomely, and by the end of production in 1962 a grand total of more than 550,000 Ponton derivatives had been built. The last of them were on sale alongside the first of the Fintail range that was introduced in late 1959 and would eventually replace them all.

MODELS: 180, 180a, 180b, 180c, 180D, 180Db, 180Dc, 190, 190b, 190D, 219, 220, 220S, 220SE.

The shape of the first Pontons was quite revolutionary for Mercedes. This is an early 180.

There were diesel Pontons, too, like this 180D. Unusually, despite the factory registration plates, this one has right-hand drive.

ENGINES: 1767cc M136 petrol four with 52PS (180); 1767cc OM636 diesel four with 40PS (180D) or 43PS (180Db); 1897cc M121 petrol four with 65PS (180a) or 68PS (180b, 180c); 1897cc M121 petrol four with 75PS (190) or 80PS (190b); 1897cc OM621 diesel four with 50PS (190D); 1988cc OM621 diesel four with 48PS (180Dc); 2195cc M180 petrol six with 85PS (220a) or 90PS from August 1957 (219); 100PS (220S) or 106PS from August 1957; 2195cc M127 injected petrol six with 115PS (220SE).

GEARBOXES: Four-speed manual, all-synchromesh. Hydrak automatic clutch optional on six-cylinders from August 1957.

SUSPENSION, STEERING & BRAKES: Front suspension with twin wishbones and

The larger 190 and 190D engines were introduced in the mid-1950s. This four-cylinder saloon dates from 1958.

coil springs. Rear suspension with swing-axles and coil springs (to September 1955, except six-cylinders) or with single-pivot swing-axles and coil springs (all six-cylinders and all others from September 1955). Recirculating-ball steering, unassisted. Drum brakes on all four wheels; vacuum servo optional from September 1955, then standard on 220S and 220SE.

DIMENSIONS: Length: 4485mm; 4500mm (four-cylinders from 1959); 4680mm (219); 4715mm (220a). **Width:** 1740mm. **Height:** 1560mm. **Wheelbase:** 2650mm (four-cylinders); 2750mm (219); 2820mm (220a). **Track:** 1430mm (front), 1475mm (rear, four-cylinders); 1470mm (rear, six-cylinders).

PERFORMANCE & FUEL CONSUMPTION: 180: 78mph, 24.5mpg, 0-100km/h in 31.0 sec; 180a, b &c: 84.5mph, 26.9mpg, 0-100km/h in 21.0 sec; 190: 86.4mph, 24.5mpg, 0-100km/h in 20.5 sec; 190b: 89.4mph, 24.5mpg, 0-100km/h in 19.0 sec; 180D & 180Db: 69.5mph, 35.3mpg, 0-100km/h in 39.0 sec; 180Dc: 74.5mph, 35.3mpg, 0-100kmh in 36.0 sec; 190D: 78.3mph, 33.2mpg, 0-100km/h in 29.0 sec; 219: 91mph, 19.5mpg, 0-100km/h in 17.0 sec; 220a: 93mph, 20mpg, 0-100km/h in 19.0 sec; 220S: 99mph, 21mpg, 0-100km/h in 17.0 sec; 220SE: 99mph, 22mpg, 0-100km/h in 15.0 sec.

PRODUCTION TOTALS: 180 (all models):

The six-cylinder 220S used a long-nose version of the Ponton bodyshell. This is a 220S model, distinguished by additional brightwork.

The long nose and absence of brightwork identify this car as a 220, or 220a as it was later known.

118,234; 190 (all models): 89,808; 180D (all models): 150,441; 190D (all models): 81,918; 219 27,845; 220a: 25,937; 220S: 55,279; 220SE: 1974.

The 219 was a hybrid, created by putting the six-cylinder engine into a short-nose bodyshell.

Visually indistinguishable from a 220S, this is the short-lived 220SE, equipped with the optional folding sunroof.

Part-built Ponton saloons were supplied to coachbuilders for completion as ambulances and other types. This ambulance was built by Miesen of Bonn.

The Fintail models, 1959-1968

The Mercedes formula for a multi-faceted range based on a single common design had worked very well for the Ponton models, and the concept was carried over when work began on their replacements. Introduced gradually from autumn 1959, these gained the nickname of Fintail types (Heckflosse in German) thanks to rear wings that hinted at the then-current American fashion for tail fins.

The Fintail design maximised interior space and its deep windows gave an airy passenger cabin. However, their major advances were in safety engineering: these were the first Mercedes to incorporate the 'crumple zone' concept with a rigid safety cell for the passengers, and interiors padded to reduce impact injuries. The 'clap-hands' windscreen wipers epitomised Mercedes' rational thinking and would become a marque

characteristic, but the vertical strip speedometer on some models was less successful. Both floor and steering column gearchanges were offered, and upholstery was in tough MB-Tex vinyl or cloth, or rarely leather.

The first Fintails were six-cylinder cars, with uprated versions of the existing 2.2-litre engine. Badged as 220 (carburettors, 95PS), 220S (carburettors, 110PS) and 220SE (injection, 120PS), they replaced the Ponton models with the same names, and were all W111 types with the vertical light clusters pioneered on the 1957 300SL Roadster. A Hydrak clutch option was offered, but was not popular.

The second tranche of releases came in 1961 with the first four-cylinders (190 and 190D, both short-nose W110 types with round lights), and a new top-model 300SE six-cylinder with a lightweight aluminium version of the injected engine from the big 300 limousines. This was a W112 type that featured an air suspension system that smoothed the ride, plus all-round disc brakes. To complicate the issue, there were 'c' suffixes for the four-cylinders and 'b' suffixes for the smaller six-cylinders to distinguish them from previous models with similar names, but these never appeared on the cars.

The new 300SE long-wheelbase model in 1963 was exactly what its name suggested. This W112 model had the same mechanical specification as the standard 300SE but an extended wheelbase helped it fill a market gap left when the big 300 limousines gave way to the new 600.

The final changes came in 1965, as enlarged four-cylinder engines produced the 200 and 200D to replace the 190 and 190D, while an enlarged six-cylinder produced the

230S to replace all the 220 models and was squeezed into a short-nose W110 body to make the new 230 model. All these final cars remained in production until 1968.

As it had done with the Pontons, Mercedes also made part-built four-cylinder Fintails available for conversion by specialists. Binz and Miesen produced ambulances and Kombi estates, and the Belgian coachbuilders Jacques Coune and IMA developed estates; the IMA types were called Universal models. Binz also worked with Mercedes to create a seven-seat airport taxi on an extended-wheelbase platform. Meanwhile, of course, the factory also offered its own two-door cabriolet and coupé derivatives, which are discussed further in Chapter 5.

These models also promoted Mercedes products through a successful rally programme between 1960 and 1965. The team cars were 220SE models for the first three years and after that 300SE models appeared alongside the 230SL sports cars.

MODELS: Saloons: 190c, 190Dc, 200, 200D, 220b, 220Sb, 220SEb, 230, 230S, 300SE, 300SE LWB; **Seven-seaters:** 200, 200D, 230; **Kombis:** 190c, 190Dc; **Universals:** 200, 200D, 230, 230S.
ENGINES: 1897cc M121 petrol four with 80PS (190c); 1988cc OM621 diesel four with 55PS (190D, 200D); 1988cc M121 petrol four with 95PS (200); 2195cc M180 petrol six with 95PS (220b); 2195cc M180 petrol six with 110PS (220Sb); 2195cc M127 petrol six with injection and 120PS (220SEb); 2281cc M180 petrol six with 105PS (230) or 120PS from 1966; (230 & 230S); 2996cc M189 petrol six with injection and 160PS or 170PS from January 1964 (300SE & 300SE LWB).
GEARBOXES: Four-speed manual, all-synchromesh. Four-speed automatic option.
SUSPENSION, STEERING & BRAKES:
Front suspension with twin wishbones, coil springs and anti-roll bar. Rear suspension with single-pivot swing axle and coil springs. Recirculating-ball steering, unassisted; optional power assistance (from May 1964 on 200 & 200D). Drum brakes on all four wheels, except 300SE & 300SE LWB; front discs from April 1962 (220S & 220SE) or August 1962 (220); disc brakes on all four wheels (300SE & 300SE LWB).
DIMENSIONS: Length: 4730mm (four-cylinders and 230); 4875mm (six-cylinders except 230); 5380mm (7-seaters). **Width:** 1795mm. **Height:** 1500mm; 1455mm (300SE & 300SE LWB). **Wheelbase:** 2700mm (four-cylinders and 230); 2750mm (220, 220S, 220SE, 230S); 2850mm (300SE LWB); 3350mm (7-seaters). **Track:** 1468mm (front) 190 &190D; 1470mm 220, 220S & 220SE;

The four-cylinder Fintails had a short bonnet and round headlamps. This one would have been rare in the UK when it was new.

The six-cylinder models had a long-nose shell and vertically stacked front lamps under a glass cover.

The tail fins were initially much larger but were toned down for production. This is a 220S.

The longer rear door of the long-wheelbase 300SE was not easy to spot in isolation.

The bright trim of the air outlet vent on the rear pillar identifies this Fintail as a 220S.

Subtle differences: extra side trim and a different air vent trim on the rear pillar marked out the 300SE.

1482mm 200, 200D,300SE & 300SE LWB; 220 (from August 1962), 220S & 220SE (from April 1962); 1485mm (rear), except 1490mm for 300SE & 300SE LWB.

PERFORMANCE & FUEL CONSUMPTION: 190 manual: 93mph, 20mpg, 0-100km/h in 18 sec; 190 automatic: 90mph, 19mpg, 0-100km/h in 22 sec; 200 manual: 100mph, 19mpg, 0-100km/h in 15 sec; 200 automatic: 98mph, 17mpg, 0-100km/h in 16 sec; 200D manual: 81mph, 26mpg, 0-100km/h in 29 sec; 200D automatic: 79mph, 23mpg, 0-100km/h in 30 sec; 220b: 99mph, 17mpg (16mpg automatic), 0-100km/h in 16 sec; 220Sb: 102mph, 17mpg (16mpg automatic), 0-100km/h in 15 sec; 220SEb: 107mph, 17mpg (16mpg automatic), 0-100km/h in 14 sec; 230 manual: 104mph, 15mpg, 0-100km/h in 14 sec; 230 automatic: 102mph, 14mpg, 0-100km/h in 16 sec; 230S manual: 109mph, 15mpg, 0-100km/h in 13 sec; 230S automatic: 108mph, 14mpg, 0-100km/h in 15 sec; 300SE (160PS): 112mph (109mph automatic), 12-14mpg, 0-100km/h in 13 sec; 300SE (170PS):

The 230S was a mid-range six-cylinder model. This one was built with right-hand-drive for the UK in 1966.

The Universal was an estate car conversion by IMA in Brussels that had Mercedes factory approval. This is a four-cylinder model.

The seven-seat airport taxi was created with the aid of the coachbuilder Binz of Lorch.

118mph (115mph automatic), 12-14mpg, 0-100km/h in 12 sec.
PRODUCTION TOTALS: (Figures include part-built models built up as ambulances and other specials.)

190c (1961-1965): 130,554; 190Dc (1961-1965): 225,645; 200 (1965-1968): 70,207; 200D (1965-1968): 161,618; 220b (1959-1965): 69,691; 220Sb (1959-1965:) 161,119; 220SEb (1959-1965): 66,086; 230 (1965-1968): 40,258; 230S (1965-1968): 41,107; 300SE (1961-1965): 5202; 300SE LWB (1962-1965): 1546.

The Stroke 8 models, 1968-1976

Few models encapsulated the Mercedes rational approach to design as well as the saloons built between 1968 and 1976. Clear thinking was evident in every mechanical element and every line – and yet they were very far from being characterless. Mercedes did struggle for a name, though, calling them its New Generation cars, but because many model designations were the same as those of the previous models, the public preferred to call them 'Stroke 8' models, referring to their 1968 introduction.

A single bodyshell for all engine types reduced the manufacturing complication of the Fintail range, despite different internal designations for the four-cylinder (W115) and six-cylinder (W114) types. Bodies were

The very neat and carefully considered lines of the Stroke 8 models are typified by this early W115 four-cylinder saloon.

Six-cylinders were not easy to identify at a glance, but the twin exhaust tailpipes of this 280E were a clue.

dimensionally similar to the Fintails but made better use of the space available. A new rear suspension with trailing arms was described as a diagonal swing-axle type to avoid making older models appear outdated, and bigger wheels allowed bigger all-disc brakes.

Even the styling seemed rational, almost geometric like the big 600 and featuring a low belt line and deep glass area. It began to look uncomfortably respectable in the changing social climate of the early 1970s, but never really dated. Inside were a superbly clean instrument layout, a centre stack, and multiple safety features that included a collapsible steering column, while buyers could once again choose from a floor or column gearchange and manual or automatic transmissions.

The programme included major derivatives. There would be part-built saloons for the specialist coachbuilders, coupé models (see p80), and a long-wheelbase eight-seat airport taxi. Plans for an estate model were shelved, allowing specialist coachbuilders to fill the gap.

The cars were introduced to the press in December 1967 and to the public at the Geneva Show in March 1968. There were two diesels (called 200D and 220D), two four-cylinder petrol types (200 and 220), and two six-cylinder petrols (230 and 250). All except the 250 had carry-over engines that had been updated. Special US models, with emissions control gear and different lighting arrangements, arrived in September. To restore the power lost to emissions requirements, the 250's engine was enlarged to 2.8 litres from summer 1970 – although the car was still called a 250.

More deliberately planned changes were made in spring 1972, when the 250's 2.8-litre single-cam engine gave way to a new M110 twin-cam 2.8-litre type; this came in a carburettor 280 model and an injected high-performance 280E. More new engines and a visual face-lift followed in autumn 1973: a third diesel model called 240D was added and a four-cylinder petrol 230 replaced the 220. To avoid confusion, the existing six-cylinder 230 was promptly renamed a 230/6. Bigger door mirrors, rain channels on the A-pillars, and ribbed tail-light lenses were the obvious features of the face-lift, along with a wider grille and flatter bonnet. All the 1974 automatics now had a floor-mounted selector and a conventional torque converter instead of Mercedes' traditional fluid flywheel.

Not finished yet, Mercedes enlarged their diesel range in summer 1974 with a remarkable five-cylinder model called the 300D in the USA but the 240D 3.0 elsewhere. This was aligned with the four-cylinder models as a W115, but in the USA it was intended as a prestige car at a time when diesel engines were becoming popular in the wake of the first oil crisis.

Production of the Stroke 8 models ended in December 1975, although assembly from CKD kits continued briefly at overseas plants. During nine years of production, more than 1.9 million of these models were built – almost as many as all previous Mercedes passenger models between 1945 and their introduction in 1968. The big sellers were always the diesels, and the least well-known derivatives the small series of ESV (Experimental Safety Vehicles) based on the Stroke 8 cars in 1971-1972.

MODELS: 200, 220, 230/4, 200D, 220D,

By the time of the Stroke 8 models diesel Mercedes saloons were in use as taxis all over the world. This one is in the standard colour used on German taxis in the 1960s and 1970s.

The long-wheelbase airport taxi version of the Stroke 8 saloons was built by Mercedes itself.

Once again, there were part-built versions of the Stroke 8 cars for specialist coachbuilders. This ambulance was built by Mercedes' regular partner, Miesen.

There were part-built models with the long-wheelbase, too. This late example was bodied as an ambulance by Binz.

220D LWB, 230, 240D, 240D LWB, 240D 3.0, 230 (230/6), 230 (230/6) LWB, 250, 280, 280E.

ENGINES: 1988cc M115 petrol four with 95PS (200); 2197cc M115 petrol four with 105PS (220); 1988cc OM615 diesel four with 55PS (200D); 2197cc OM615 diesel four with 60PS (220D); 2277cc M115 petrol four with 110PS (230/4); 2292cc M180 petrol six with 120PS (230 & 230/6); 2376cc OM616 diesel four with 65PS (240D); 2496cc M114 petrol six with 130PS (250, to 1969); 2778cc M130 petrol six with 130PS (250 & 250 2.8, 1969-1972); 2746cc M110 DOHC six with 160PS (280); 2746cc M110 DOHC six with 185PS and fuel-injection (280E); 2971cc OM617 diesel five with 80PS (240D 3.0).

GEARBOXES: Four-speed manual standard. Five-speed manual optional on six-cylinders. Four-speed automatic.

SUSPENSION, STEERING & BRAKES: Front suspension with twin wishbones, coil springs and anti-roll bar. Rear suspension with 'diagonal swing axle' (semi-trailing arms), coil springs, rubber auxiliary springs and anti-roll bar. Optional hydro-pneumatic self-levelling strut. Recirculating ball steering; optional power assistance. Disc brakes on all four wheels.

DIMENSIONS: Length: 4680mm. **Width:** 1770mm. **Height:** 1440mm. **Wheelbase:** 2750mm. **Track:** 1448mm (front), 1440mm (rear).

PERFORMANCE & FUEL CONSUMPTION: 200D: 81mph, 35mpg, 0-100km/h in 31.0 sec (manual), 78mph, 0-100km/h in 33.5 sec (automatic); 220D: 83mph, 33mpg, 0-100km/

17

h in 29.0 sec (manual), 80mph, 0-100km/h in 30.0 sec (automatic); 200 101mph, 26mpg, 0-100km/h in 16.0 sec (manual), 98mph (automatic); 220: 104mph, 25mpg, 0-100km/h in 14.0 sec (manual), 101mph (automatic); 230/4: 106mph, 24.5mpg, 0-100km/h in 14.0 sec; 103mph (automatic); 230 & 230/6: 110mph, 25mpg, 0-100km/h in 14.0 sec (manual), 107mph (automatic); 240D: 86mph, 30mpg, 0-100km/h in 25.0 sec (manual), 83mph (automatic); 240D 3.0: 93mph, 26mpg, 0-100km/h in 20.0 sec (manual), 90mph, 0-100km/h in 21.0 sec (automatic); 250: 115mph, 24mpg, 0-100km/h in 13.0 sec (manual), 112mph (automatic); 280: 118mph, 23mpg, 0-100km/h in 11.0 sec; 280E: 124mph, 23mpg, 0-100km/h in 10.0 sec.

PRODUCTION TOTALS: Figures are for all models except coupés, and include CKD, LWB and part-built types where applicable. 200: 288,775; 200D: 339,927; 220: 128,732; 220D: 420,070; 230 (four-cyl): 87,785; 230/6: 221,713; 240D: 131,319; 240D 3.0/300D: 53,690; 250: 78,303; 250 (2.8): 34,061; 280: 44,537; 280E: 11,518.

The W123 models, 1976-1985

The 123-series cars that replaced the Stroke 8 models once again had saloons as the core of the range, but the coupé, part-built and long-wheelbase derivatives were accompanied for the first time by estate models.

The overall design was made as flexible as possible to accommodate future changes in US lighting and safety requirements, and a key aim was to reduce servicing costs. Front and rear suspensions were bolted directly to the bodyshell but otherwise very similar to their W116 counterparts, and the all-disc braking system had standard servo assistance and a tandem safety system.

Friedrich Geiger's stylists created a design with a slightly wedge-shaped lower body and simple, elegant lines with a family resemblance to the W116 S-Class. Four-cylinder models were given paired round headlamps and fog lamps, while six-cylinder cars had rectangular headlamps and additional chrome trim.

The three-dial instrument panel of the R107 SL and W116 S-Class was adapted, but there was still a US-style foot-operated parking brake except for RHD models, which had a twist-grip type under the dashboard. All manual gearboxes had a floor change, but automatics could have either column or floor-mounted change levers. The W123s also gained conventional windscreen wipers that covered around 20% more of the screen than the earlier clap-hands type.

The new range was announced in 1976 in saloon form only. Coupés, the long-wheelbase variants and the part-built types would all appear during 1977, and the estates were delayed until 1978 while Mercedes converted its Bremen factory from its former light commercial work.

The nine models announced at the Geneva Show in 1976 ran from 200D to 280E. Eight had updated versions of engines in the earlier saloons, the ninth being a completely new six-cylinder 2.5-litre petrol type that created the new 250 model. They

The styling of the 123 range was extremely well resolved. This is a six-cylinder 280E with right-hand-drive for the UK, where the cars sold strongly.

The rear view was as good as the front. This is another 280E model.

The T-model estates were styled at the same time as the saloons and there was no awkwardness about their longer rear ends.

were an immediate success, and waiting times for a new W123 soon reached 12 months or more.

Demand was still strong when the estate models were added in April 1978. Mercedes called them T-models, the 'T' standing for Transport and Tourism, and the letter T would form part of their model designations. There were five variants at first, a four-cylinder 230T, six-cylinder 250T and 250TE types, and diesel 240TD and 300TD models.

There were only minor improvements and specification adjustments before February 1979, when the 220D was dropped and the 200D and 240D both gained extra power. Bigger changes were held over until that autumn, when the second major phase of 123-series production began.

The second-series changes were introduced over an extended period, and were largely invisible. However, there were new lightweight M102 four-cylinder petrol engines for the 200 and 230 models, a more powerful six-cylinder for the 250, and new manual gearboxes for all the four-cylinder cars. A sixth estate model was also

announced, although it did not become available until autumn 1980 and then only in Germany and the USA. This was the 300TD Turbodiesel, with a turbocharged version of the five-cylinder OM617 engine. Meanwhile, in April the carburettor 230T was replaced by an injected 230TE, and in November a 200T with the new M102 engine was added.

The 1981 models brought stronger body shells and an improved heating and ventilating system, while the top model 280E gained a new four-speed automatic gearbox and ABS became optional. At the end of the 1981 season, the carburettor 280 models were dropped, the revised 250 providing their replacement. The 1982 models reflected that year's Energy Concept programme with fuel-saving measures and new gearboxes. From January 1982 a driver's airbag became an extra-cost option, and then in April that year the millionth diesel 123 saloon came off the lines at Sindelfingen.

The two millionth saloon model (the total included those one million diesels) was celebrated in September 1982, just in time for the start of the 1983 model-year and the opening of the third major phase in 123-series production. These third-series cars all had rectangular headlamps, together with some minor changes and interior alterations. The new four-speed automatic gearbox was now progressively introduced, and then for 1984 engine and gearbox changes brought the four-cylinder models into line with the new compact W201 range.

The last changes anticipated new emissions requirements in Germany, as the last diesel models gained a Diesel Particulates Filter during 1985 and a catalyst-equipped 230E became available. Production ran down gradually: the last saloon was built in November but the estates lingered until January 1986, while CKD assembly in South Africa continued for a couple of months longer than that. Even then, the 123 was not quite finished, and an assembly operation opened in China and lasted until 1988.

The overall total of 123-series models is normally quoted as 2.7 million. This figure represented major success for Mercedes, and the vindication of its decision to introduce estate models, which would now figure as

Turbocharging was becoming widely used as a way of getting better performance; this S123 estate has the five-cylinder turbocharged diesel engine.

part of every new medium-saloon range from the company.

MODELS: Saloons: 200 (M115), 200 (M102), 230, 230E, 250, 250 LWB, 280, 280E, 200D, 220D, 240D, 240D LWB, 300D, 300D LWB, 300D Turbodiesel (USA). **Estates:** 200T, 230T, 230TE, 250T, 280TE, 240TD, 300TD, 300TD Turbodiesel (USA).

ENGINES: 1988cc OM615 diesel four with 55PS (200D); 1988cc M115 petrol four with 94PS (200 to 1980); 1997cc M102 petrol four with 109PS (200 from 1980); 2197cc OM615 diesel four with 64PS (220D); 2299cc M102 petrol four with 136PS and fuel-injection (230E, 230TE); 2307cc M115 petrol four with 109PS (230, 230T); 2404cc (quoted as 2399cc from August 1978) OM616 diesel four with 65PS (240D, 240TD); 2525cc M123 petrol six with 129PS or 140PS from September 1979 (250, 250T); 2746cc M110 DOHC petrol six with 156PS (280); 2746cc M110 DOHC petrol six with 177PS and fuel-injection or 185 PS from 1978 (280E, 280TE); 2998cc (quoted as 3005cc until August 1978) OM617 diesel five with 80PS or (from September 1979) 88PS (300D, 300TD); 2998cc OM617 turbocharged diesel five with 125bhp (300D Turbodiesel & 300TD Turbodiesel for USA).

GEARBOXES: Four-speed manual standard. Five-speed manual optional from February 1982. Four-speed automatic.

SUSPENSION, STEERING & BRAKES: Front suspension with twin wishbones, coil springs, hydraulic telescopic dampers and

US traffic and safety regulations in this period demanded new solutions. The lights on this six-cylinder car are similar to those on European four-cylinders, and there are extended bumpers as well.

There was an airport taxi in the range again, neatly styled but very obviously on an extended wheelbase.

anti-roll bar. Rear suspension with semi-trailing arms, coil springs, hydraulic telescopic dampers and anti-roll bar; hydro-pneumatic self-levelling optional on saloons and standard on estates and long-wheelbase models. Recirculating-ball steering, unassisted; power assistance optional, standard on some models, then standard on all models from September 1982. Disc brakes on all four wheels, with servo assistance and dual hydraulic circuit; ABS optional from August 1980.

DIMENSIONS: Length: 4725mm. **Width:** 1786mm. **Height:** 1438mm (saloon); 1471mm (estate). **Wheelbase:** 2795mm. **Track:** 1488mm (front), 1446mm (rear).

PERFORMANCE & FUEL CONSUMPTION: 200: 99mph, 17.5mpg, 0-100km/h in 15 sec; 200: (M102) 105mph, 19mpg, 0-100km/h in 14 sec; 200D: 81mph, 35mpg, 0-100km/h in 31 sec; 220D: 83mph, 23.5mpg, 0-100km/h in 29 sec; 230: 105mph, 18mpg, 0-100km/h in 13 sec; 230E: 112mph, 18mpg, 0-100km/h in 12 sec; 240D: 86mph, 19.5mpg, 0-100km/h in 20 sec; 250: 112mph, 16mpg, 0-100km/h in 12 sec; 280: 118mph, 15mpg, 0-100km/h in 10.5 sec; 280E: 124mph, 15mpg, 0-100km/h in 10 sec; 300TD Turbodiesel: 102mph, 17mpg, 0-100km/h in 15 sec.

PRODUCTION TOTALS: Petrol saloons (1976-1985): 1,091,601. Diesel saloons (1976-1985): 1,283,839. LWB saloons, all types (1977-1985): 13,700. Petrol estates (1978-1986): 95,521. Diesel estates (1978-1986): 103,996. Platforms, all types (1976-1985): 8373.

The 124 models, 1984-1996

Mercedes' next new saloon range was drawn up alongside the new compact W201 models in the late 1970s, and had deliberate similarities. The new 124 series models also had a close relationship to the larger S-Class models of the 126 series. All were styled by Bruno Sacco with careful attention to aerodynamics and a family resemblance, and the 124 models were the last to go on sale.

This was an immensely complicated model range. There were W124 saloons, S124 estates, C124 two-doors (see p93), V124 LWB models, F124 part-built models and VF124 part-built LWB models. Most types had sub-variants, not least to meet US regulations, and some models were supplied in CKD kit form for overseas assembly.

The cars had the same front strut and five-link rear suspension as the W201s, and the range offered the usual choice of petrol and diesel engines (and later petrol V8s as well). An increased use of plastics in the 124s' construction saved weight and reduced fuel consumption, while interiors were typically sober, but also modern in feel and appearance.

The saloons were announced at Frankfurt in 1984 and deliveries began in early 1985. There were four petrol models and three diesels. The four-cylinder engines in the 200E and 230E belonged to the still-new M102 family, while the brand-new six-cylinders in the 260E and 300E were impressively powerful and efficient, and the three diesels

Part-built 123 models on both wheelbases were available for the specialists. This ambulance was built by Miesen on the long wheelbase.

(200D, 250D and 300D) were four-, five- and six-cylinder variants of a common design. Automatic gearboxes came with switchable Standard and Economy modes.

The new 124s were an immediate success and quickly supplanted the W201s as Mercedes' best-seller, and by the time estate models arrived in autumn 1985 there were waiting lists of up to two years. Estates were both neatly styled and extremely capacious, all being lower-geared to compensate for their extra weight. Alongside them, Mercedes announced new (though optional) traction aids and the 4Matic automatic four-wheel-drive system for some models, although deliveries of the latter did not begin until early 1987.

The US models introduced in summer 1985 had minimal differences from their European counterparts – ugly headlamp units were the most obvious ones. The first emissions-controlled engines for Europe also became available, catalyst-equipped KAT or catalyst-prepared RÜF versions of all models except the carburettor 200 being offered. The first part-built models for specialist bodywork, with both standard and long wheelbases,

appeared in 1986, and the coupés (see p93) would be added in 1987. This massively comprehensive range then continued until mid-1989 with only minor changes, the most important of which were the standardisation of ABS brakes in September 1988 and the addition of 250D Turbodiesel models.

With the second-generation models in autumn 1989 came distinctive lower flank panels similar to those on the coupés, plus bright trim highlights and body-colour mirror bodies. There was more interior wood and seats were now more supportive. The new Sportline option and the 150mph 300E-24 model with four-valve 3-litre engine headlined changes intended to counter rivalry from BMW. A year later would come the 500E, a limited-volume V8 model assembled under contract by Porsche, and in 1991 the 400E with 4.2-litre V8 would capitalise on that car's success; these engines would only ever be used in saloons. In late 1989, long-wheelbase six-door limousines were introduced, and 1991 saw cabriolets added to the two-door range (see p94).

The third-generation cars were introduced

Bumpers were partly concealed behind aprons on the 124-series cars; this example is an early saloon.

gradually in 1992 and 1993, new four-valve petrol engines for both four-cylinder and six-cylinder models arriving in autumn 1992 along with five-speed automatics for the sixes and the option of new eight-hole alloys on all models. From autumn 1993, a minor face-lift brought a recessed front grille, and new four-valve diesel engines were introduced. The focus on sporty models increased as AMG-tuned types were added to the catalogue, too. At the same time, the cars were rebranded as E-Class types, and designations changed. As examples, the 200E became an E200 and the 250D an E250 Diesel, but an anomaly was that the 400E became an E420.

Production began to wind down in March 1995, as a gradual changeover to the new W210 range began, although CKD models were supplied to India until June 1996. By the time production had ended, the total of 124-series models had exceeded 2.7 million, of which by far the most numerous was the 230E saloon.

MODELS: Saloons: 200, 200D, 200E, 220E, 230E, 250D, 250D Turbodiesel, 260E, 280E, 300D, 300D Turbodiesel, 300E, 300E-24, 320E, 400E, 500E, E200, E200 Diesel, E220, E250 Diesel, E250 Turbodiesel, E280, E300 Diesel, E300 Turbodiesel, E320, E36 AMG, E420, E500, E60 AMG. **Estates:** 200T, 200TD, 200TE, 220TE, 230TE, 250TD, 250TD Turbodiesel, 280TE, 300TD, 300TD Turbodiesel, 300TE, 300TE-24, 320TE, E200, E220, E250 Diesel, E280, E300 Diesel, E300

The chamfer on the rear wings was added to improve aerodynamics. This is an early 200D model.

The companion T-model estates were again a major visual success. This one has the optional alloy wheels.

Turbodiesel, E320, E36 AMG.

ENGINES: (All petrol engines had injection except the M102 four-cylinder in the 200 and 200T models, which used carburettors). 1997cc M102 petrol four with 109PS or 105PS (KAT) (200, 200T); 1997cc M102

The 1989 mid-life face-lift brought plastic flank panels, as seen on this S124 estate.

Models for the USA still required special headlamps, but the new bumpers had been drawn up to meet local regulations and looked the same for all countries.

petrol four with 122PS or 118PS (KAT) (200E, 200TE); 1998cc M111 DOHC petrol four with 136PS (200E, 200TE); 2199cc M111 DOHC petrol four with 150PS (220E, 220TE); 2299cc M102 petrol four with 136PS or 132PS (KAT) (230E, 230TE); 2599cc M103 petrol six with 166PS or 160PS (KAT) (260E); 2962cc M103 petrol six with 190PS or 185PS (KAT) (300E,300TE); 1997cc OM601 diesel four with 72PS or (from February 1989) 75PS (200D, 200TD, E200 Diesel); 2497cc OM602 diesel five with 90PS or (from February 1989) 94PS (250D, 250TD); 2497cc OM602 turbocharged diesel five with 126PS (250D Turbodiesel, 250TD Turbo); 2497cc OM605

DOHC diesel five with 113PS (E250 Diesel); 2799cc M104 DOHC petrol six with 197PS or (from July 1993) 192PS (280E, 280TE); 2960cc M104 DOHC petrol six with 220PS (300E-24, 300TE-24); 2996cc OM603 diesel six with 109PS or (from February 1989) 113PS (300D, 300TD); 2996cc OM603 turbocharged diesel six with 143PS or (from September 1988) 147PS (300D Turbodiesel, 300TD Turbodiesel); 2996cc OM606 DOHC diesel six with 136PS (E300 Diesel); 3199cc M104 DOHC petrol six with 220PS (320E, 320TE); 3604cc M104 DOHC petrol six with 272PS (E36 AMG); 4196cc M119 petrol V8 with 279PS (400E, E420); 4973cc M119 petrol V8 with 326PS or (from October 1992) 320PS (500E, E500).

GEARBOXES: Four-speed manual, to 1992. Five-speed manual. Five-speed close-ratio manual, from 1989. Four-speed automatic. Five-speed automatic, from 1990.

SUSPENSION, STEERING & BRAKES: Front suspension with MacPherson struts, wishbones, coil springs and anti-roll bar. Rear suspension with five links, coil springs and anti-roll bar; hydro-pneumatic self-levelling strut standard on estates and 500E/E500, and optional on other models. Sportline lowered suspension option from late 1989. Power-assisted recirculating-ball steering. Disc brakes all round, ventilated on some models;

This 1994 E200 model has the recessed radiator grille and the late type of moulded plastic wheel trims.

dual hydraulic circuit and servo assistance; ABS initially optional, then standard from September 1986 on six-cylinder petrol models and from September 1988 on all models.

DIMENSIONS: Length: 4740mm (saloons); 4765mm (estates). **Width:** 1740mm. **Height:** 1446mm (saloons to October 1988, and all 4Matics); 1431mm (saloons from November 1988, except 4Matics); 1490mm (estates, over roof bars). **Wheelbase:** 2800mm. **Track:** 1497mm (front), 1488mm (rear), except 400E/E420 & 500E/E500 1501mm (front), 1491mm (rear) for 400E/E420 or 1518mm (front) and 1509mm (rear), with Sportline 1538mm (front), 1529mm (rear) for 500E/E500.

PERFORMANCE & FUEL CONSUMPTION: Figures shown are for non-KAT models except where a KAT was standard. Estate models were typically around 8mph slower than saloons and took around 0.7 sec longer to reach 100km/h.

200: 113mph, 30mpg, 0-100km/h in 13.1 sec; 200D: 99mph, 34mpg, 0-100km/h in 18.5 sec; 200E (M102): 118mph, 29mpg, 0-100km/h in 11.8 sec; 200E (M111): 121mph, 27mpg, 0-100km/h in 12 sec; 220E: 127mph, 27mpg, 0-100km/h in 10.6 sec; 230E: 123mph, 29mpg, 0-100km/h in 10.4 sec; 250D: 106mph, 30mpg, 0-100km/h in 17 sec; 250D Turbodiesel: 121mph, 29mpg, 0-100km/h in 12.3 sec; 260E: 132mph, 24mpg, 0-100km/h in 9.5 sec; 280E/E280: 140mph, 23mpg, 0-100km/h in 8.9 sec; 300D: 115mph, 29mpg, 0-100km/h in 14.1 sec; 300D Turbodiesel: 125mph, 29mpg, 0-100km/h in 10.9 sec; 300E: 140mph, 24mpg, 0-100km/h in 8.3 sec; 300E-24: 144mph, 22mpg, 0-100km/h in 7.8 sec;

320E: 143mph, 22mpg, 0-100km/h in 7.8 sec; 400E/E420: 155mph (limited), 21mpg, 0-100km/h in 7.2 sec; 500E: 155mph (limited), 19mpg, 0-100km/h in 6.1 sec; E250 Diesel: 116mph, 30mpg, 0-100km/h in 16 sec; E300 Diesel: 122mph, 31mpg, 0-100km/h in 13 sec; E36 AMG: 155mph, 22mpg, 0-100km/h in 7.0 sec; E60 AMG: 155mph, 19mpg, 0-100km/h in 5.4 sec.

PRODUCTION TOTALS: 200: 110,354; 200D/E200 Diesel: 236,926; 200E (M102): 176,660; 200E/E200 (M111): 82,588; 200T: 7467; 200TD: 7373; 200TE (M102): 20,555; 200TE/E200 estate: 15,279; 220E/E220: 105,346; 220TE/E220 estate: 22,057; 230E: 374,422; 230E Platform: 224; 230E LWB Platform: 711; 230TE: 64,945; 250D: 236,811; 250D LWB: 776; 250D LWB: Platform 2331; 250D Platform: 741; 250D Turbodiesel/E250 Turbodiesel: 48,876; 250TD: 43,628; 250TD Turbo/ E250 Turbodiesel estate: 4745; E250 Diesel: 41,411; E250 Diesel estate 15,625; E250 Diesel LWB: 181; E250 Diesel Platform: 301; E250 Diesel LWB Platform: 642; 260E: 154,391; 260E 4Matic: 1943; 260E LWB: 1,006; 260E LWB Platform: 1049; 280E/ E280: 57,302; 280E/E280 LWB: 379; 280E/ E280 LWB Platform: 399; 280TE/E280 estate: 12,177; 300D: 131,647; 300D 4Matic: 1485; 300D Turbodiesel/E300 Turbodiesel: 38,908; 300D Turbodiesel 4Matic/E300 Turbodiesel 4Matic: 2136; 300E: 258,063; 300E-24: 19,300; 300E 4Matic/E300 4Matic: 14,202; 300TD: 21,901; 300TD Turbo/E300 Turbodiesel estate: 14,844; 300TD Turbo 4Matic/E300 Turbodiesel 4Matic estate: 2317; 300TE: 41,775; 300TE-24: 6282; 300TE 4Matic/E300 4Matic: 12,094; E300 Diesel: 23,166; E300 Diesel estate: 9071; 320E/ E320: 63,950; 320TE/E320 estate: 18,368; E36 AMG estate included in 320TE/E320 estate total; 400E/E420: 22,802; 500E/E500: 10,479; AMG E60 included in 500E/E500 total.

Looking suitably powerful with its widened wheelarches, this is the E500 model with a 5-litre V8 engine.

The long-wheelbase 124 models came with six doors, and were typically described as limousines rather than airport taxis.

W210 E-class, 1995-2003

Major changes of Mercedes policy affected the design of the W210 models. Most had been prompted by the success of rival BMW models, and there was a new focus on reducing manufacturing costs and on meeting customer demands. New thinking on specifications also led to a hierarchy of trim levels in preference to a long options list.

The 210 range introduced a new look with paired oval lamps and more rounded body contours. This is an early E230 Classic saloon.

Unfortunately, the new emphasis on cost-saving was apparent in small details, and build-quality issues that became apparent early on took several years to cure. The desire to keep Mercedes products fresh through more frequent model changes also ensured that the W210s would have a shorter production life than the 124-series models they replaced. The W210 range was less comprehensive than its predecessor, too, because there were no coupé or cabriolet derivatives.

The W210s were more curvaceous than the W124 models, with better aerodynamics, extra width and a longer wheelbase to give more cabin room. They were the first production Mercedes to have the new front end with twin oval headlamps, a style that was repeated on the tail light lenses.

The new range was announced in June 1995, with nine engines that were mostly carried over from the 124 range and uprated as necessary. Saloons and estates alike had both petrol and diesel options, but the E420 V8 top model came only as a saloon and was not available until February 1996 and then not in all countries. The hierarchy of trim levels was the same as already seen on the W202 C-class: Classic, Elegance and Avantgarde.

The first AMG-tuned car arrived in May 1996 as an E36 AMG with the M104 six-cylinder from the 124 range, but this gave way

in January 1997 to the V8-powered E50 AMG. Both models were visually and physically much closer to the mainstream models than their 124-series predecessors had been.

New at the Geneva Show in 1997 was an E430 to replace the E420, featuring one of the new modular V8 engines. A 4Matic drivetrain (extensively redesigned from the 124-series type) became an option for bigger-engined models, and both Brake Assist and a service interval indicator became available. More changes soon followed, and the 1998-model 210s introduced in autumn 1997 included new V6 petrol engines and an E55 AMG with the new V8 to replace the E50 AMG model. Five-speed electronically controlled automatic gearboxes arrived, and so did the only supercharged W210, the E200 Kompressor model.

The range was already a huge success and the 210s led their class by June 1998 when the 1999 models were announced with Mercedes' first common-rail diesel engines. The new OM611 four-cylinder had only one capacity of 2151cc, but electronic controls allowed differently tuned versions to power the new E200 CDI and E220 CDI. These new diesel models were however not sold in the USA.

The oval theme was continued on the lenses of the tail lights, as seen on this early E300 Turbodiesel.

The estate derivatives were another visual success. This one is a UK-market E430 model, with V8 engine.

The rear view of the same estate shows the softer, rounded lines of the 210 range to advantage.

The mid-life face-lift brought several front-end changes to the 210 range, as seen on this 2001 saloon.

A subtle mid-life face-lift in 1999 brought narrower headlamps and a new apron spoiler. There were more conventional rear light lenses, reshaped door mirrors with turn indicator repeaters, and, inside, a new multi-function steering wheel and a larger dashboard display screen. Two more common-rail diesel models were added – the five-cylinder E270 CDI and the six-cylinder E320 CDI – and the four-cylinder E220 CDI was uprated from 125PS to 143PS.

These changes were the last of major significance before production began to wind down in the first quarter of 2002, as saloon models were discontinued one by one. The estates remained in production until March 2003, and the CKD assembly operations in Egypt, India and Mexico were also closed to make way for the new W211 E-class. In all, 1,374,409 W210s were built.

MODELS: Saloons: E200, E200 CDI, E200 Diesel, E200 Kompressor, E220 CDI, E220 Diesel, E230, E240 (2398cc), E240 (2597cc), E250 Diesel, E250 Turbodiesel, E270 CDI, E280 (M104), E280 (M112), E290 Turbodiesel, E300 Diesel, E300 Turbodiesel, E320 (M104), E320 (M112), E320 CDI, E36 AMG, E420, E430, E50 AMG, E55 AMG. **Estates:** E200, E200 Kompressor (Italy, Greece, Portugal), E220 CDI (2151cc), E220CDI (2148cc), E230, E240 (2398cc), E240 (2597cc), E250 Diesel, E250 Turbodiesel, E270 CDI, E280, E280 4Matic, E290 Turbodiesel, E300 Turbodiesel, E320, E320 4Matic, E320 CDI, E420, E430, E430 4Matic, E55 AMG, E55 AMG 4Matic.

ENGINES: 1997cc OM604 diesel four with 88 PS (E200 Diesel); 1998cc M111 petrol four with 136 PS or 163PS (E200); 1998cc M111 supercharged petrol four with 192 PS (E200 Kompressor); 2148cc OM611 diesel four with 116 PS (E200 CDI); 2148cc OM611 diesel four with 143PS (E220 CDI); 2151cc OM611 diesel four with 102 PS (E200 CDI); 2151cc OM611 diesel four with 125 PS (E220 CDI); 2155cc OM604 diesel four with 95PS (E220 Diesel), also Biodiesel-ready version with 75PS; 2295cc M111 petrol four with 150 PS (E230); 2398cc M112 petrol V6 with 170 PS (E240); 2497cc OM605 diesel four with 113 PS (E250 Diesel); 2497cc OM605 turbocharged diesel four with 150 PS (E250 Turbodiesel); 2597cc M112 petrol V6 with 170PS (E240); 2685cc OM612 diesel five with 170 PS (E270 CDI); 2799cc M104 petrol six with 193 PS (E280); 2799cc M112 petrol V6 with 204 PS (E280); 2874cc OM602 turbocharged diesel five with 129 PS (E290 Turbodiesel); 2996cc OM 606 diesel six with 136 PS (E300 Diesel); 2996cc OM 606 turbocharged diesel six with 177 PS (E300 Turbodiesel); 3199cc M104 petrol six with 220 PS (E320); 3199cc M112 petrol V6 with 224 PS (E320); 3222cc OM613 diesel six with 197 PS (E320 CDI); 3606cc M104 petrol six with 272PS (E36 AMG); 4196cc M119 petrol V8 with 279 PS (E420); 4266cc M113 petrol V8 with 279 PS (E430); 4973cc M119 petrol V8 with 347 PS (E50 AMG); 5439cc M113 petrol V8 with 354 PS (E55 AMG).

GEARBOXES: Five-speed manual (to 1999). Six-speed manual (from 1999). Four-speed automatic (to 1996). Five-speed automatic (from 1996).

SUSPENSION, STEERING & BRAKES: Front suspension with twin wishbones, coil springs, and anti-roll bar. Rear suspension with five links, coil springs, and anti-roll bar. Hydropneumatic self-levelling optional. Rack-and-pinion steering with power assistance. Disc brakes all round, ventilated at the front, with servo assistance, ABS and (from March 1997) Brake Assist.

DIMENSIONS: Length: 4795mm (saloons to 1999); 4818mm (saloons from 1999); 4816mm (estates to 1999); 4839mm (estates from 1999); 5553mm (LWB models to 1999); 5576mm (LWB models from 1999). **Width:** 1799mm. **Height:** 1411-1441mm. **Wheelbase:** 2833mm; 3570mm (LWB). **Track:** 1528-1542mm (front), 1528-1543mm (rear).

PERFORMANCE & FUEL CONSUMPTION: E220 CDI: 132mph, 45mpg, 0-100km/h in 10.4 sec (manual); E230: 131mph, 25mpg, 0-100km/h in 8.9 sec; E240: 138mph, 27.5mpg, 0-100km/h in 9.6 sec (manual); E270 CDI: 133mph, 39mpg, 0-100km/h in 9.5 sec (manual); E280 (M112): 143mph, 32mpg, 0-100km/h in 9.1 sec (auto); E320 (M104): 146mph, 22mpg, 0-100km/h in

7.8 sec (auto); E320 CDI: 143mph, 35mpg, 0-100km/h in 8.3 sec; E430: 155mph (limited), 26mpg, 0-100km/h in 6.6 sec; E55 AMG: 155mph (limited), 23mpg, 0-100km/h in 5.7 sec.

PRODUCTION TOTALS: These figures do not include the part-built models.

	Saloons	Estates
E200:	144,362	12,900
E200 CDI:	48,573	
E200 Diesel:	688	
E200 Kompressor:	15,432	7100
E220 CDI:	94,531	32,100
E220 Diesel:	64,531	
E230:	109,527	10,773
E240:	94,455	29,200
E250 Diesel:	14,520	1500
E250 Turbodiesel:	11,262	2253
E270 CDI:	45,600	21,900
E280 (M104):	25,548	4000
E280 (M112):	41,311	
E280 4Matic:	5318	3800
E290 Turbodiesel:	53,191	20,100
E300 Diesel:	27,834	
E300 Turbodiesel:	53,437	15,712
E320 (M104):	99,043	
E320 (M112):	187,137	44,200
E320 4Matic:	33,292	18,900
E320 CDI:	33,643	19,900
E420:	31,159	2903
E430:	46,461	4600
E430 4Matic:	7722	1300
E50 AMG:	2960	
E55 AMG:	10,073	1700.

Bodykit and wheels mark this out as a high-performance E55 AMG estate.

The 300 Models, 1951-1962

Rare in the UK, this 1953 300 model is representative of the original cars.

This 300b variant differs from the original 300 mainly in the addition of a bright metal spat on the rear wing.

The 300 name is carried below the boot lid, and the bright metal housing above the rear wing houses a turn signal light.

Few cars have ever demonstrated the determination of their manufacturers better than the Mercedes-Benz 300 that made its bow at the Frankfurt Motor Show in April 1951. It delivered a powerful message: Mercedes was back in business and was willing and ready to supply prestigious cars to heads of state around the world. The launch event was carefully chosen, too, because the 1951 Frankfurt Show was West Germany's first major international motor show of the postwar period, as important in its own way as the 1948 Geneva Show had been for the rest of Europe.

The 300 was a large and formal luxury saloon, built on Mercedes' favoured cruciform backbone-type chassis scaled up to an appropriate size. Under its imposing bonnet was the company's latest overhead-valve six-cylinder engine with a 2996cc capacity and an output of 115PS that could propel the car to 100mph if given a long enough stretch of road, and would provide autobahn cruising at 80-90mph when required. All-round independent suspension with coil springs and a long 120in wheelbase guaranteed a very high standard of ride comfort that was supplemented by a ride-selection arrangement at the rear.

The standard saloon body bore a strong family resemblance to that of the contemporary 220S, but was deliberately styled to look big and imposing. It was no surprise that the 300 was adopted by the German Federal Government for official duties, and, in fact, became so closely associated with that role that it gained the popular nickname of the Adenauer Mercedes, after Konrad Adenauer, the first Chancellor of the Federal Republic.

For more formal duties there was the four-door Cabriolet D, a parade car in the great Mercedes tradition that was mainly sold outside Germany.

The injected 300d had multiple differences, including squared-off rear wings and inset fog lights. It was also a pillarless design, as displayed here.

Also unsurprising was that Mercedes developed several derivative models. There were luxury cabriolets, coupés and roadster models in the 300S range, and these are discussed from page 77. On the full-size saloon chassis there was the Cabriolet D – really a parade car that picked up on a prewar Mercedes tradition and was very much a hand-finished and formidably expensive machine destined primarily for export. This was announced at the same time as the saloon in 1951 but did not enter production until March 1952.

Between 1951 and 1957, the 300 was a W186 model, and was improved incrementally in the usual Mercedes fashion. The biggest change was to a single-pivot swing-axle rear suspension in 1955. However, the car was given a major overhaul in 1957, becoming a 300d type with sharper, more modern styling and a fuel-injected engine. As usual, the 300d designation was internal, and badges simply read '300', but this car was very different from its predecessors.

Visually, the main changes were extended rear wings and a re-profiled roof with wraparound rear window, plus pillarless construction that allowed all windows to be lowered completely into the doors. The injected engine came from the 300SL sports car and promised 160PS and enough torque to make

The Cabriolet D was updated along with the saloon when the injection engine was introduced. These cars were always rare.

Not many 300s had special bodywork, but Binz turned this one into an ambulance for Switzerland.

an automatic transmission standard (it had been introduced as an option on the 300c two years earlier). In practice, weight had gone up and the top speed of the 300d was not much higher than that of its predecessors, although the servo-assisted drum brakes were by this stage worryingly anachronistic.

The 300 was a worthy flagship for Mercedes in the 1950s, despite its shortcomings. Replacing it required a very special effort, and there was a hiatus after production ended in May 1962 while the factory prepared for the magnificent 600 that was to succeed it.

MODELS: 300 (1951-1954); 300b (1954-1955); 300c (1955-1957); 300d (1957-1962).

ENGINE: 2996cc M186 petrol six with 115PS (300), or 125PS (300b & 300c); 2996cc M189 petrol six with 160PS and fuel-injection (300d).

GEARBOX: Four-speed all-synchromesh manual. Three-speed automatic optional on 300c & 300d.

STEERING, SUSPENSION & BRAKES: Twin wishbones at the front, with coil springs and anti-roll bar; swing axles at the rear with coil springs; electric rear ride control. Recirculating-ball steering. Drum brakes on all four wheels, with servo assistance.

DIMENSIONS: Length: 4950mm (300); 5065mm (300b & 300c); 5190mm (300d). **Width:** 1840mm; 1860mm (300d). **Height:** 1640mm (300 & 300b); 1600mm (300c); 1620mm (300d). **Wheelbase:** 3050mm; 3150mm (300d). **Track:** 1480mm (front); 1525mm (rear).

PERFORMANCE & FUEL CONSUMPTION: 300: 99mph, 14mpg, 0-100km/h in 18.0 sec; 300b: 101mph, 14.7mpg, 0-100km/h in 17.0 sec; 300c manual: 99mph,14.7mpg, 0-100km/h in 17.0 sec; 300c auto: 96mph, 14mpg, 0-100km/h in 18.0 sec; 300d manual: 105mph, 14mpg, 0-100km/h in 17.0 sec; 300d auto: 102mph, 13mpg, 0-100km/h in 18.0 sec.

PRODUCTION TOTALS: 300 & 300b: 6214 saloons, including 12 bare chassis and 591 Cabriolet D. 300c: 1432, including 3 bare chassis and 51 Cabriolet D. 300d: 3077, including one bare chassis, 65 Cabriolet D.

The 600, 1963-1981

By the end of the 1950s, Mercedes was ready to make a bid for the very top of the global car market and to pour all its engineering expertise into one glorious automotive statement. The result, four years in the making, arrived as the W100 600 at the Paris Motor Show in 1963, although production for sales did not begin until a year later.

The 600 creamed off the top of the market for the earlier 300 limousine, while the new 300SE catered for the lower end of that market. From the start, the 600 was positioned as the car for celebrities, statesmen, royalty and emperors, and it was priced accordingly. Although the cars would always be hand-built to order, there were two core models from the beginning. These were a five-seater, intended largely for the owner-driver, and a seven-seater on an extended wheelbase, called the 600 Pullman. Later, there would be additional models on the long-wheelbase – a landaulet with alternative short and long-roof configurations, and a six-door alternative to the standard four-door model. Some would have divisions, and some would be armour-plated.

The 600 or 'Grosser' model made a powerful statement about Mercedes' engineering abilities – and about the wealth of the owner.

Even the standard-wheelbase car was enormous, with a vast and capacious boot. (Alexander Migl, CC-by-SA 4.0)

The 600 made its point in the USA, too, where all models had to have a special headlamp configuration. (Vic Dorn/Public Domain)

The W100 was an engineering tour de force, a huge monocoque structure with front and rear sub-frames to support the running-gear, and the same dependence on a passenger safety-cell protected by crumple zones as the smaller Mercedes of the time. It ran on height-adjustable air suspension and was packed with luxury and convenience features, many of them driven by a high-pressure hydraulic system. Window lifts, seat adjustment, central locking, fuel filler cap and scuttle air vent were all silently operated by hydraulics, as were the division and sunroof when these options were fitted. Air-conditioning was also (perhaps surprisingly) an option, but power-assisted steering and brakes were standard.

The long-wheelbase model was known as a Pullman model. This is the four-door variant.

The power unit was a brand-new iron-block 6.3-litre V8 engine called the M100, which came with Bosch injection and was rated at 250PS. It was able to power this heavy car to nearly 130mph in standard-wheelbase form and to ensure that acceleration was even better than that of the contemporary 300SE models. A four-speed automatic gearbox was the only option, and disc brakes all round made for safe stopping power.

The styling drew on existing Mercedes models, perhaps most obviously on that of the Fintail saloons with which the 600 shared its

The six-door variant of the Pullman; these were much rarer than the four-door type.

vertically-stacked front lights and somewhat geometric appearance. It was at its best on the long-wheelbase variants, the abundance of chrome trim tending to make the standard-

There were landaulet bodies for the long-wheelbase 600, too. This one was specially built for the Pope.

Another special 600, and this time one of only two coupés built for senior members of the company.

wheelbase models look a little heavy and over-dressed. Nevertheless, its main point was to impress, and that was something it achieved effortlessly. As a state limousine, parade landaulet, or simple demonstration of wealth and status, the 600 was simply unequalled.

The interior design, too, shared cues with other Mercedes of the time. The instrument panel had neat circular dials like those in the prestigious cabriolet and coupé models of the time; there was an abundance – for some tastes too much – of figured wood trim; and upholstery was in hard-wearing perforated leather, although a cloth option was available and was favoured in some of the hotter countries to which the 600 was exported. On the long-wheelbase models, even the third row of seats was fully upholstered when many rival limousines still depended on folding occasional seats. Curtains for the rear side windows, hat nets, and headrests were all part of the standard specification.

The 600 was never a strong seller, and

nor was it ever intended to be. Its purpose was less to make profits for Mercedes than to demonstrate the company's engineering and manufacturing abilities. Nor did the model ever really date in nearly two decades of production. Mercedes decided to withdraw the car from sale in the USA at the end of the 1972 season rather than attempt to make it meet ever-tightening emissions control legislation, and sales took a further hit globally after the oil crisis of the early 1970s. Nevertheless, the last car was not built until June 1981, its 18-year production run being the longest of any Mercedes model up to that point.

Probably no two examples of the Mercedes 600 were exactly alike, but in addition to the 'standard' production models there were also a few special derivatives. A pair of coupé models built for senior Mercedes engineers had a two-door version of the design on a shortened wheelbase, and a single landaulet was built from a standard-wheelbase car for an aristocratic German racing driver. Another standard-wheelbase model was customised by the French coachbuilder Henri Chapron in 1966, when Mercedes itself declined to meet its owner's wishes.

The 600 was never replaced, either directly or indirectly. Mercedes probably concluded that the cost of developing such a car was far too great and that there were more important projects to which it should devote its resources. For that reason, the 600 stands alone in the Mercedes canon, admired as much today as it was in its lifetime – if not more so.

MODELS: 600 (1964-1981); 600 Pullman (1964-1981).
ENGINE: 6330cc M100 injected V8 with 250PS.
GEARBOX: Four-speed automatic.
SUSPENSION, STEERING & BRAKES: Front suspension with wishbones, and anti-roll bar. Rear swing-axle suspension with single joint and low pivot, self-levelling air springs, and auxiliary rubber springs. Recirculating-ball steering with power assistance. Disc brakes all round, with servo assistance.
DIMENSIONS: Length: 5450mm; 6240mm for Pullman. **Width:** 1950mm. **Height:**

1500mm; 1510mm for Pullman. **Wheelbase:** 3200mm; 3900mm for Pullman. **Track:** 1587mm (front), 1581mm (rear).
PERFORMANCE & FUEL CONSUMPTION: 600: 128mph, 12mpg, 0-100km/h in 10 sec; 600 Pullman: 124mph, 11mpg, 0-100km/h in 12 sec.
PRODUCTION TOTALS: 600: 2190; 600 Pullman: 304; Pullman 6dr: 124; Landaulet: 59.

The W108 & W109 Models, 1965-1971

Mercedes' development of a broad Fintail model-range meant that the most expensive 300SE models were close visual relatives of the 180D types found on taxi-ranks around the world. Stuttgart clearly began to worry that this might deter potential buyers of the top models, and decided to develop a distinctive body style for its more expensive saloons.

This was based on the Fintail floorpan, but the plan was to use only the larger six-cylinder engines together with high levels of standard equipment. There would be W108 models on the standard wheelbase and W109 models on a lengthened wheelbase, and an S after the model name – supposedly standing for Super –

would help to ensure exclusivity. Unfortunately, introducing a 230S derivative of the Fintail range in the mid-1960s rather undermined the plan, and ensured that these cars would not usually be known by the S-Class name applied to their successors.

Paul Bracq designed the new body, and unsurprisingly took several cues from his acclaimed cabriolet and coupé designs for the Fintail models. His new four-door saloon was long, low, and wide, again with a large glass area and the vertical front light units already associated with the more expensive Mercedes models. It had a notably substantial look, along with a more spacious passenger cabin, and its clear and attractive cowled instrument binnacle was again inspired by the example of the two-door models. To those unaware of the link, it was hardly credible that all this concealed the essentials of a Fintail saloon.

The first of the new models arrived in 1965 and defined the scope of the range. The two lower-priced cars were W108s with the new 2.5-litre engine, a 250S with carburettors and a more expensive 250SE with injection. Above these came a 300SE on the standard wheelbase, with the existing injected 3-litre light-alloy engine, and then at the top of the range was a long-wheelbase W109 model with that same engine, badged as a 300SEL and

Although based on an evolution of the Fintail saloon platform, the 250SE looked like a much bigger car.

The combination of straight-through lines with gentle curves produced a highly attractive shape.

There was no hint at all that these cars were related to the Fintails, which were beginning to date by the time they arrived. This is a 250SE.

The top-model 300SEL with its longer wheelbase and additional brightwork also had air suspension.

featuring air suspension. Production of the Fintail 300SE and its long-wheelbase variant was halted to make way for the newcomers.

The second-generation models of the W108 and W109 ranges became public in autumn 1967, when the existing engines were replaced by several different versions of a new 2.8-litre type called the M130. The 280S and 280SE replaced the 250S and 250SE, and there was a new long-wheelbase model called the 280SEL. It was at this point that the traditional Mercedes model-naming system dependent on engine size began to break down, because a higher-powered version of the same engine also went into the new 300SE and 300SEL models in place of the older light-alloy type. The two 300s were, of course, distinguished by higher equipment levels as well, and both of them had air suspension.

There were, in fact, six 1968 model-year introductions, the sixth arriving in December 1967 and being a complete outlier that nobody had expected. Mercedes engineer Erich Waxenberger had enjoyed some racing success by putting the 6.3-litre V8 from the 600 limousine into a W108 shell, and the results had been impressive enough for Mercedes to risk a production model with that specification. The 300SEL 6.3 had the best of everything, with the air-sprung long-wheelbase bodyshell and its 250PS engine driving through an automatic gearbox. It looked standard, except for fatter tyres and stacked halogen headlamps; it was always very expensive, but there was nothing else quite like this high-performance luxury saloon at the time, and sales certainly exceeded Mercedes' expectations.

From then on, all new models in the W108 and W109 ranges would have V8 engines, but this was a period in which US emissions controls requirements were emerging as a factor in engine design and the result was a slightly confusing range of cars. Mercedes introduced its new 3.5-litre M116 V8 in late

Adding the new V8 engine produced a 300SEL 3.5, which always had the twin stacked headlamps shown here.

The 300SEL 6.3 concealed its identity very well, although the boot-lid badge revealed that this had the big V8 engine from the 600 limousine.

1969 for the flagship model of the mainstream range, which now became a 300SEL 3.5. (In line with this 'flagship model' policy, it was made available in the coupé and cabriolet models at the same time.)

A year later, the same engine went into the other two models of the mainstream range, creating a 280SE 3.5 and a 280SEL 3.5. These remained on sale outside the USA until production ended in 1972. In the USA, however, the only way to maintain performance in the face of tightening emissions controls was by using another V8 engine, this time with a 4.5-litre size and called the M117. Despite a whole extra litre of capacity, it produced only the same 200PS as the existing 3.5-litre type. So for the 1972 season, the USA received models called 280SE 4.45, 280SEL 4.5, and (with air suspension) 300SEL 4.5.

These complications would be resolved when the next new generation of top Mercedes saloons was released in 1972 as the W116 S-Class, now taking on the name that had been tentatively but never wholeheartedly applied to the W108s and W109s.

MODELS: 250S, 250SE, 280S, 280SE, 280SE 3.5, 280SE 4.5, 280SEL, 280SEL 3.5, 280SEL 4.5, 300SE (M189), 300SE (M130), 300SEL (M189), 300SEL (M130), 300SEL 3.5, 300SEL 4.5, 300SEL 6.3.
ENGINES: 2496cc M108 petrol six with

130PS (250S); 2496cc M108 injected petrol six with 150PS (250SE); 2778cc M130 petrol six with 140PS (280S); 2778cc M130 injected petrol six with 160PS (280SE & 280SEL); 2778cc M130 injected petrol six with 170PS (300SE & 300SEL from 1968); 2996cc M189 injected petrol six with 170PS (300SE & 300SEL to 1967); 3499cc M116 injected petrol V8 with 200PS (280SE 3.5, 280SEL 3.5 & 300SEL 3.5); 4520cc M117 petrol V8 with 200PS (280SE 4.5, 280SEL 4.5 & 300SEL 4.5, USA); 6330cc M100 injected petrol V8 with 250PS (300SEL 6.3).
GEARBOXES: Four-speed manual. Five-speed manual optional from 1968 on 280SE. Four-speed automatic optional; standard on 300SEL 6.3. Three-speed automatic standard on 4.5 models.

SUSPENSION, STEERING & BRAKES: Front suspension with wishbones, coil springs and anti-roll bar. Rear swing-axle suspension with single joint and low pivot, coil springs and hydraulic self-levelling. Recirculating-ball steering; power assistance optional. Disc brakes all round, with servo assistance.
DIMENSIONS: Length: 4900mm; 5000mm for LWB models. **Width:** 1810mm; 1440mm over mirrors. **Height:** 1400mm. **Wheelbase:** 2750mm; 2850mm for LWB models. **Track:** 1482mm (front), 1485mm (rear) or 1490mm for LWB models.
PERFORMANCE & FUEL CONSUMPTION: 250S manual: 113mph, 18mpg, 0-100km/h

in 13 sec; 250S automatic: 110mph, 17mpg, 0-100km/h in 13 sec; 250SE manual: 120mph, 18mpg, 0-100km/h in 12 sec; 250SE automatic: 117mph, 18mpg, 0-100km/h in 12 sec; 280S manual: 115mph, 17.5mpg, 0-100km/h in 12 sec; 280S automatic: 112mph, 17mpg, 0-100km/h in 12 sec; 280SE manual: 120mph, 17.5mpg, 0-100km/h in 11 sec; 280SE automatic: 117mph, 17mpg, 0-100km/h in 11 sec; 280SE 3.5: 130mph, 15mpg, 0-100km/h in 10 sec; 300SE (M189): 121-124mph, 15-17mpg, 0-100km/h in 12 sec; 300SEL (M130): 121mph, 17mpg, 0-100km/h in 11 sec; 300SEL 6.3: 137mph, 13mpg, 0-100km/h in 8 sec.

PRODUCTION TOTALS: 250S: 74,677; 250SE: 55,181; 280S: 93,666; 280SE: 91,051; 280SEL: 8250; 280SE 3.5: 11,309; 280SEL 3.5: 951; 280SE 4.5: 13,527; 280SEL 4.5: 8173; 300SE (M189): 2737; 300SEL (M189): 2369; 300SEL (M130): 2519; 300SEL 3.5: 9583; 300SEL 4.5: 2553; 300SEL 6.3: 6526.

The W116 range took the S-Class name and consolidated Mercedes as leader of the luxury saloon sector. This is a 280SE. (Beck Wiesbaden 2008, GNU Free Documentation Licence)

The rear view of the same 280SE shows the ribbed tail light lenses characteristic of the model. (Beck Wiesbaden 2008, GNU Free Documentation Licence)

The W116 S-Class, 1972-1980

The **W116** saloons, the first cars to be formally called S-Class models, were as much a demonstration of Mercedes' abilities as the 600 had been back in 1963 – but this time they brought that demonstration down to a more affordable level. Design and development took six years, and the cars were introduced at the 1972 Paris Salon.

Like all Mercedes of their era, the cars were ruthlessly rational in conception. Their design was also heavily influenced by US environmental and safety requirements, and in addition to the usual safety cell construction they incorporated several ideas pioneered on the experimental safety vehicles of the early 1970s. These features not only made them heavier than their W108 and W109 predecessors, but also reduced interior space slightly because of the additional safety padding.

From the beginning, the cars were designed with US market variants in mind, as well as overseas assembly (which took place in Venezuela); they were also designed to have both standard and long-wheelbase derivatives. The trailing-arm rear suspension was very similar to that on the Stroke 8 saloons, while the front suspension was designed for a wide engine bay and was mounted on a lightweight cross-tube rather than a full sub-frame. The body design by Friedrich Geiger combined long and low lines with an imperious stance, and was refined in a wind tunnel.

The first European models were the 280S, 280SE and 350SE, with improved versions of the twin-cam 2.8-litre six and the 3.5-litre V8.

Longer rear doors in the long-wheelbase variants blended perfectly with the overall proportions. This is a 450SEL.

Fuchs alloy wheels, as seen on this standard-wheelbase car, were a popular option.

US Federal models followed about six months later with a 450SE powered by the 4.5-litre V8 and burdened with extended bumpers and twin round headlamps. At about the same time a 450SE and long-wheelbase 450SEL were introduced to Europe as new top models. The 450SEL, with an extra 100mm in its wheelbase, won the 1974 European Car of the Year title, and the long-wheelbase models would later be made available in 350SEL and 280SEL guise as well.

The 1973 oil crisis delayed plans for the flagship 450SEL 6.9, with a big-bore version of the 600's 6.3-litre V8 engine, but the car was announced in 1974 and sales began in May 1975. This top model came with multiple luxury options and with hydro-pneumatic suspension as standard. The engine drove through a three-speed automatic gearbox and the car could reach 140mph, making it just faster than a V12 Jaguar of the time. The car would become a favourite of racing drivers and other celebrities.

Sales in the USA were only a small proportion of the total, but Mercedes was determined to persevere. To conserve costs, changes needed to keep the W116 saleable were generally standardised worldwide. From November 1975, the new tunable Bosch K-Jetronic injection system eased one problem, even though the need for catalytic converters and special Californian requirements continued to cause complications.

From 1976, a new Automatic Climate Control option based on a Chrysler system helped keep the W116 in the US game. More

US regulations once again required round headlamps and extended bumpers, and Mercedes gambled on success with the diesel engine in this 300SD.

significant was the availability from May 1978 of a special diesel W116 for the USA only. The 300SD was intended to bring down the average fuel consumption of Mercedes cars in the USA, and so to avoid fines under the CAFE (Corporate Average Fuel Economy) legislation. It had a turbocharged version of the existing five-cylinder diesel engine coupled to an automatic gearbox.

October 1978 brought the announcement of exciting new technology in the form of a Bosch ABS system. This was made available worldwide on the W116, although its additional cost limited the take-up rate. More minor changes followed in mid-1979 to meet the 1980-season US regulations, but these would be the last. The final W116 was built at Mercedes' Sindelfingen factory in September 1980, and was a North American 300 SD.

Discreet and anonymous, unless the badges were visible; the legendary 450SEL 6.9 was the rocket-ship saloon of its day.

Small numbers of these saloons were armoured, and some of the conversions had Mercedes approval. However, the company always restricted its own models to standard and long-wheelbase saloons, so that further variations were left to aftermarket specialists. Over the years, these met demand for versions with extended wheelbases (some with six doors), for estate models, and even for hearses. In later years, and into the 1980s, there were also bolt-on bodykits – some of them exhibiting dubious taste – to individualise the cars.

MODELS: 280S, 280SE, 280SEL, 300SD, 350SE, 350SEL, 450SE, 450SEL, 450SEL 6.9.

ENGINES: 2746cc M110 petrol six with 160PS or 156PS from 1976 (280S); 2746cc M110 injected petrol six with 185PS or (1976-1978); 177PS (280S & 280SEL), 2998cc OM617 turbocharged diesel five with 115PS (300SD); 3499cc M116 petrol V8 with 200PS, or (1976-1978) 195PS, or (from 1978) 205PS (350SE & 350SEL); 4520cc M117 petrol V8 with 225PS, or (1975-1976) 217PS; (450SE & 450SEL); 6834cc M100 petrol V8 with 286PS (450SEL 6.9).

GEARBOXES: Four-speed manual (280 & 350 models only). Five-speed manual (280 & 350 models only). Three-speed automatic (350, 450 and 6.9). Four-speed automatic (280 & 300SD).

SUSPENSION, STEERING & BRAKES: Front suspension with wishbones, coil springs with auxiliary rubber springs, and anti-roll bar. Rear suspension with semi-trailing arms, coil springs with auxiliary rubber springs, and anti-roll bar; optional self-levelling strut. 450SEL 6.9 with self-levelling hydro-pneumatic springs all round, and anti-roll bars front and rear. Recirculating-ball steering, with standard power assistance. Disc brakes all round, ventilated on front wheels; twin hydraulic circuits and servo assistance; ABS optional from 1979.

DIMENSIONS: Length: 4960mm; 5220mm (US models); 5060mm (SEL models). **Width:** 1870mm. **Height:** 1425mm; 1430mm (SEL models). **Wheelbase:** 2865mm; 2965mm (SEL models). **Track:** 1521mm (front), 1505mm (rear).

PERFORMANCE & FUEL CONSUMPTION: 280S manual: 118mph, 17.5mpg, 0-100km/h in 10.5 sec; 280S automatic: 118mph, 17.5mpg, 0-100km/h in 11.5 sec; 280SE manual: 124mph, 17.5mpg, 0-100km/h in 10.5 sec; 280SE automatic: 124mph, 17.5mpg, 0-100km/h in 11.5 sec; 300SD: 102mph, 20mpg, 0-100km/h in 17 sec; 350SE manual: 127mph, 15mpg, 0-100km/h in 10 sec; 350SE automatic: 127mph, 15mpg, 0-100km/h in 11 sec; 450SE: 130mph, 15mpg, 0-100km/h in 10.5 sec; 450SEL 6.9: 140mph, 13mpg, 0-100km/h in 8 sec.

PRODUCTION TOTALS: 280S: 122,848; 280SE: 150,593. 280SEL: 7032. 300SD: 28,634. 350SE: 51,100. 350SEL: 4266. 450SE: 41,604. 450SEL: 59,578. 450SEL 6.9: 7380.

Smoother and sleeker than their predecessors, the W126 models initially had ribbed lower flank panels.

The W126 S-Class, 1979-1992

The major influence on the W126 replacements for the W116 S-Class models was the focus on fuel economy that followed the 1973 oil crisis. As a result, when the new models arrived at the Frankfurt show in September 1979 they had much-improved aerodynamics, lighter weight, and new engines that were more fuel-efficient.

These cars established the family look of the 1980s Mercedes. Styling was by Bruno Sacco, who had drawn up both standard- and long-wheelbase saloons as well as coupé derivatives (see p90). There were deliberate resemblances to the earlier W116, but the shape was strikingly clean and appeared smaller and lighter too. Key features included ribbed flank protection panels (a Sacco trademark) and deformable bumper aprons that met US regulations. An Econometer now figured within the established instrument panel design.

There were four launch models: six-cylinder 280 S (carburettor) and 280 SE (injection) types, and 380 SE and 500 SE models with new all-alloy V8 engines. The long-wheelbase 500SEL was shown at Frankfurt but not sold until June 1980. North American customers had to wait until January 1981 for their two-model range, which consisted of a standard-wheelbase 300SD (with a further developed version of the W116's diesel engine) and a long-wheelbase 380SEL. A 500SEL would follow for the

Yet again there were special headlamps for the USA, but this time the bumpers were carefully blended into the overall styling.

USA in 1983. Careful design minimised the differences between European and US models, but the US cars needed special headlamp units to meet local regulations. There was also one slip-up: the bore and stroke of the 3.8-litre V8s had to be changed to meet US emissions requirements, making them different from the European engines.

Further improvements in fuel economy came from engine and gearbox developments announced with the Energy Concept programme at Frankfurt in 1981. At the same time, a driver's airbag and passenger's seatbelt tensioner became options, and the European 3.8-litre engines were revised to share the dimensions developed for the US models. The range of 280S, 280SE, 280SEL, 380SE, 380SEL, 500SE, 500SEL and US 300SD then remained unchanged until mid-1985.

The 1985 Frankfurt show introduced

The face-lifted 126 models had smooth flank panels and, as here, flat-faced wheel trims to reduce aerodynamic drag.

The top model 560SEL had the long-wheelbase bodyshell, a 5.6-litre V8 engine, and smooth-faced alloy wheels as standard.

The W126 was used by police forces in some parts of Germany. This late model has the characteristic green and white police livery.

extensive revisions. Smooth flank panels refreshed the appearance, there were more new engines, and the European cars were made available with catalytic converters in anticipation of new German regulations for 1986. Switchable automatic gearboxes were introduced, along with 15in wheels on low-profile tyres. Three new six-cylinder models (260 SE, 300 SE and 300 SEL) had the new M103 all-aluminium engines introduced

earlier in the W124 saloons, while 420SE and 420SEL models replaced the 3.8-litre cars. The 500SE and 500SEL incorporated improvements, and a new top-of-the-range 560SEL had a long-stroke derivative of the big V8 and performance (limited to 155mph) that surpassed that of the old 450SEL 6.9.

Not shown at Frankfurt, but nevertheless important, was a new model for the USA called the 300SDL, which combined the long-wheelbase body with the latest six-cylinder OM603 diesel engine from the latest Mercedes family of 'modular' diesels. This lasted only until autumn 1987.

Mercedes probably intended W126 production to end in 1988 or 1989, but the arrival of a new V12 engine from BMW disrupted the programme. Mercedes scurried off to design its own V12 for the planned replacement models. As a result, the life of the W126 range was extended.

September 1988 brought body-colour flank panels and a 560SE model that was available only in Germany. Then from June 1989 a 3.5-litre development of the OM603 diesel engine went into a new 350SDL model for the USA and a year later into a companion standard-wheelbase 350SD. There were no more changes of real significance, and W126 production began to wind down at the start of 1990. It was, nevertheless, a slow process, and the very last W126, a 560 SEL, was not built until April 1992.

Of the 818,036 W126 S-Class saloons built in 12 years, just under 12% had diesel engines; that percentage would increase with subsequent S-Class ranges. Mercedes had built few special variants, the most numerous being armoured types, but the W126 was on sale during a boom period for the aftermarket conversions industry. AMG, still an independent tuning company, provided high-performance options, and several German specialists created hugely expensive and sometimes outlandish custom rebuilds for customers who were mainly in the Middle East.

MODELS: 260SE, 280S, 280SE, 280SEL, 300SD, 300SDL, 300SE, 350SD, 350SDL, 380SE, 380SEL, 420SE, 420SEL, 500SE, 500SEL, 560SE, 560SEL.

ENGINES: 2599cc M103 petrol six with 166PS or 160PS with KAT (260SE); 2746cc M110 petrol six with 156PS (280S); 2746cc M110 injected petrol six with 185PS (280SE & 280SEL); 2962ccc M103 petrol six with 188PS or 180PS with KAT; (300SE); 2996cc OM603 turbocharged diesel six with 150PS (300SDL); 2998cc OM617 turbocharged diesel five with 125PS (300SD); 3449cc OM603 turbocharged diesel six with 136PS (350SD &; 350SDL); 3818cc (3839cc from 1981) M116 petrol V8 with 218PS, or (from 1981) 204PS; 157PS on early US models (380SE & 380SEL); 4196cc M116 petrol V8 with 218PS, or 231PS from September 1987; 204PS with KAT, or 224PS from September 1987 (420SE & 420SEL); 4973cc M117 petrol V8 with 240PS, or 231PS from spring 1981, or 245PS from September 1985, or 265PS from; September 1987; 223PS with KAT, or 252PS from September 1987 (500SE & 500SEL); 5547cc M117 petrol V8 with 300PS; 279PS with KAT (560SE & 560SEL).

GEARBOXES: Four-speed manual standard on six-cylinder models to spring 1981. Five-speed manual standard on six-cylinder petrol models from spring 1981. Four-speed automatic optional on six-cylinder petrol models; standard on all diesel and V8 models.

SUSPENSION, STEERING & BRAKES: Front suspension with wishbones, coil springs with auxiliary rubber springs and anti-roll bar. Rear suspension with semi-trailing arms, coil springs with auxiliary rubber springs, and anti-roll bar; optional self-levelling strut. Recirculating-ball steering with standard power assistance. Disc brakes all round, ventilated on front wheels and solid on rears; twin hydraulic circuits and vacuum servo assistance; ABS optional (standard on 500 and 560 models).

DIMENSIONS: Length: 4955mm; 5135mm (LWB models); 5020mm (USA); 5160mm (USA LWB models). **Width:** 1820mm. **Height:** 1436mm; 1440mm (LWB models). **Wheelbase:** 2935mm, except 2930mm (500SE); 3075mm (LWB), except: 3070mm (500SEL). **Track:** 1545mm (front), 1517mm (rear).

PERFORMANCE & FUEL CONSUMPTION: 260SE: 127mph, 21mpg, 0-100km/h in 10.2 sec; 280S: 124mph, 15.5mpg, 0-100km/h in 12 sec; 280SE: 130mph,

15.5mpg, 0-100km/h in 11 sec; 300SD: 102mph, 16mpg, 0-100km/h in 16 sec; 300SDL: 121mph; 300SE: 127mph, 21mpg, 0-100km/h in 9.4 sec; 350SDL: 109mph; 380SE: 133mph, 18mpg, 0-100km/h in 9.5 sec; 420SE: 137mph, 22mpg, 0-100km/h in 8.7 sec; 500SE: 146mph, 20mpg, 0-100km/h in 7.2sec; 560SEL: 155mph (limited), 18.5mpg, 0-100km/h in 6.8 sec.

PRODUCTION TOTALS: 260SE: 20,836; 280S: 42,996; 280SE: 133,955; 280SEL: 20,656; 300SE: 105,422; 300SEL: 40,956; 300SD: 78,726; 300SDL: 13,830; 350SD: 2066; 350SDL: 2925; 380SE: 58,239; 380SEL: 27,014; 420SE: 13,996; 420SEL: 74,017; 500SE: 33,418; 500SEL: 72,693; 560SE: 1252; 560SEL: 75,071.

The W140 S-Class, 1991-1998

The W140 S-Class range never really recovered from an unfortunate start to life. Very much products of the 1980s economic boom, these were large cars that were designed to parade their owners' wealth. A delayed launch saw their introduction coincide with the start of a recession. These saloons and their companion coupés (see p96) therefore appeared to be out of touch with their times, and were a major factor in the subsequent re-thinking of Mercedes' engineering and model strategies.

The range was also planned as a technological tour de force that would demonstrate its maker's abilities. That was reflected in its wealth of special features, such as double glazing, power-close doors,

The W140 looked big and heavy, and deliberately so. Unfortunately, it was out of step with its times.

This late S500 model has a different wheel design and colourless lenses for the rear turn indicators.

The face-lift did make the cars look a little smaller, but not much. This one shows the clear front indicator lenses that were becoming fashionable.

The long-wheelbase models were of course even bigger, but wore their extra length well. This is a V12-engined S600 with the early rear end design.

automatic climate control and a data bus linking the multiple electronic systems. A hugely spacious passenger cabin was central to the W140 design, and only careful exterior styling by Bruno Sacco's team prevented the cars' overall size being more apparent, and gave them a respectable drag coefficient. Even then, the styling was not a complete success, with bulky front and rear ends, characterless deep flanks, and an untidy dropped waistline. The 140-series nevertheless set a new style for the 1990s Mercedes with its grille set into the bonnet panel.

The mechanical underpinnings were less unusual, with a twin-wishbone front suspension and a five-link rear type, both mounted on sub-frames. Top models added a hydro-pneumatic levelling system with adjustable dampers. There was a new speed-variable power steering system, and the disc brakes were ventilated all round except on entry-level models.

Released in October 1991, the first W140s came in standard- and long-wheelbase forms, and with five different engines. The four petrol types were a 300SE six-cylinder, 400SE and 500SE V8s, and the flagship 600SE with a V12 engine. Development of this all-alloy engine had been the main cause of the W140's delayed introduction: when Mercedes learned that BMW was planning a V12, it initiated a crash programme to develop its own. The fifth engine was a turbocharged six-cylinder diesel, which powered the 350SD model for the USA. The petrol model-names were not accurate reflections of engine size but indicated the range hierarchy: the 300SE was actually a 3.2-litre, for example (and in the USA the model was badged 300SE 3.2).

An early priority was to make the 140 saloons appear smaller than they were, but the redesign took time. Meanwhile, planned new models helped customer perceptions, and in October 1992 an entry-level 280SE (300SE 2.8 in the USA) and a European diesel 300SD (much as the US 350SD) were added. The new model naming policy now confused the issue, and from June 1993 the cars were rebadged from S280 up to S600.

The S-Class was presented as a slimmer, leaner car at the February 1994 Geneva Show. Subtle changes drew attention to its width rather than height and also reduced the apparent bulk of the front end – although the V12 gained its own distinctive grille. Headlamps were uprated, and bichromatic lenses tidied the rear light units. Then from May 1995, the new Parktronic distance-sensing radar became an option, and standard on the S600.

September 1995 brought mainly incremental changes. The V8 and V12 models took on adaptive five-speed automatic gearboxes, while the ESP electronic stability programme became optional on the V8s and standard on the V12s. Announced at

And yet longer! This was the six-door Pullman model that was introduced late in the production run.

the same time, but not on sale for another year, was the S600 Pullman (coded V140), an extended-wheelbase model that was a deliberate piece of one-upmanship. A full metre longer than the long-wheelbase model, it had a six-window configuration, came with an array of convenience extras, and could also be armoured.

There was then another makeover for the 1997 model-year, when the plastic flank panels were painted in the body colour. Front side airbags became standard, while rain-sensing windscreen wipers and Xenon headlamps with dynamic range adjustment added new technology. At the same time, a more powerful diesel engine created the S300 Turbodiesel model.

W140 saloon production ended in summer 1998, by which time 406,532 cars had been built in just seven seasons. A few more Pullman models were completed in 1999 and the final seven in 2000. The annual average of just over 58,000 a year made clear just how much customers had turned against the big Mercedes when compared to the 88,000 a year achieved by the W126 models. Even impeccable build standards and top-quality design had not been able to save the W140 from being the wrong car for its time.

MODELS: The LWB identifier on post-1993 models was not included as part of the badging.

S280, 300SD (USA), S300 Turbodiesel, 300SE 2.8 (USA), 300SE, 300SEL, S320, S320 LWB, S350 Turbodiesel, 400SE, 400SEL, S420, S420 LWB, 500SE, 500SEL, S500, S500 LWB, 600SE, 600SEL, S600, S600 LWB, S600 Pullman.

ENGINES: 2799cc M104 petrol six with 193 PS (300SE 2.8 & S280); 2996cc OM606 turbocharged diesel six with 177PS (S300 Turbodiesel); 3199cc M104 petrol six with 231 PS (300SE, 300SEL, S320 & S320 LWB); 3449cc OM603 diesel six with 150 PS (300SD); 3449cc OM603 turbocharged diesel six with 150 PS (S350 Turbodiesel); 4196cc M119 petrol V8 with 286 PS, or (from 1992) 279PS (400SE, 400SEL, S420 & S420 LWB); 4973cc M119 petrol V8 with 326PS, or (from 1992) 320PS (500SE, 500SEL, S500 & S500 LWB); 5987cc M120 petrol V12 with 408PS, or (from 1992) 394PS (600SE, 600SEL, S600 & S600 LWB, S600 Pullman).

GEARBOXES: Five-speed manual (six-cylinder models only). Four-speed automatic (to 1995) Five-speed automatic (from 1995).

SUSPENSION, STEERING & BRAKES: Front suspension with twin wishbones, coil springs, and anti-roll bar. Rear suspension with five links, coil springs, and anti-roll bar. Self-levelling rear suspension optional on all petrol models, and adaptive damping optional with it; hydro-pneumatic suspension optional on V8 models and standard on V12 models.

Recirculating-ball steering with variable ratio and power assistance. Disc brakes all round, ventilated at the front only on 300SE and 300SEL and ventilated all round on other models: standard ABS, with power assistance.

DIMENSIONS: Length: 5113mm, 5213mm (SEL/LWB) or 6213mm (Pullman). **Width:** 1886mm. **Height:** 1497mm or 1495mm (with hydro-pneumatic suspension). **Wheelbase:** 3040mm, 3140mm (SEL/LWB) or 4140mm (Pullman). **Track:** 1602mm (front), 1574mm (rear).

PERFORMANCE & FUEL CONSUMPTION: S300 Turbodiesel: 128mph, 30mpg, 0-100km/h in 11.2 sec; S350 Turbodiesel: 115mph, 25mpg, 0-100km/h in 13.1 sec; S280: 130mph, 23mpg, 0-100km/h in 11 sec; S320: 140mph, 24mpg, 0-100km/h in 8.9 sec; S420: 152mph, 25mpg, 0-100km/h in 8.3 sec; S500: 155mph (limited), 22mpg, 0-100km/h in 7.3 sec; S600: 155mph (limited), 19mpg, 0-100km/h in 6.6 sec; S600 Pullman: 130mph (limited).

PRODUCTION TOTALS: S280: 22,784; S320: 98,095; S320 LWB: 85,346; S300 Turbodiesel: 7583; S350 Turbodiesel: 20,518; S420: 14,277; S420 LWB: 35,191; S500: 21,942; S500 LWB: 65,065; S600: 3399; S600 LWB: 32,517.

The W220 S-Class, 1998-2005

With the W220 range that followed the W140s, Mercedes' top priority was to win back lost customers. Design priorities were that the cars should look sleeker and lighter without sacrificing cabin room, and that they should actually be lighter as well. The car that resulted was a brilliant success, not only winning back for Mercedes the leadership of the luxury saloon market but also earning global praise for its curvaceous good looks. The companion C215 luxury coupé (see p100) similarly reversed the failure of the C140 models.

Clever packaging gave the W220 more cabin room within a shorter overall length than its predecessor, and multiple airbags in a wraparound interior design improved safety. Pioneering new technologies such as a new automatic climate control system helped to set the car apart from rivals. A new AIRmatic electronically-controlled air suspension improved the ride, while strategic use of HLA steel, aluminium and plastics both reduced weight and added strength to the body. Packaging restrictions prompted the use of power-assisted rack-and-pinion steering, but this also contributed to improved driving dynamics. Meanwhile, turn signal repeaters

Mercedes recovered its design leadership with the sleek W220 models. The shaped front light units were a very distinctive feature.

Bright-finish alloy wheels were an obvious element in the make-up of the S600 model.

in the door mirror bodies proved to be an influential innovation.

The W220 was announced at the 1998 Paris show. The initial release consisted of three petrol models, badged S320, S430, and S500. All of them came in both standard and long-wheelbase forms, and all their engines were variants of the latest three-valve Mercedes design, with a V6 in the S320 and V8s in the other two. By the end of the year there was also a V6-engined S280, available only with the shorter wheelbase. US buyers nevertheless had to wait until mid-1999 for the new models, and received only S430 and S500 types.

New variants now followed thick and fast. The anticipated AMG derivative arrived in March 1999 as an S55 AMG, sharing its engine with other Mercedes-AMG models. But probably the most important model of all was the S320 CDI, the first diesel model in the range, which was launched in November 1999 and added new levels of refinement to diesel frugality, earning it a strong following. The V12 model promised at the 1998 launch made its debut in January 2000 with the brand-new M137 engine as an S600 (despite its 5.8-litre capacity) in long-wheelbase form only, and of course was added to the range in the USA as well. Then in summer 2000, a new twin-turbo diesel V8 was introduced to make the S400 CDI, a model mainly intended to counter the new V8 diesels from Audi and BMW, and not sold in all markets.

The high-performance S55 AMG retained a discreet appearance despite its special front apron.

Quad tailpipes and special alloy wheels helped to mark out the high-performance AMG saloon.

It was also during 2000 that Mercedes added extended-wheelbase Pullman and armoured long-wheelbase variants of the S500 and S600. The last new model in this

There was, of course, a long-wheelbase model, seen here in S600 guise and in right-hand-drive form for the UK.

phase of W220 production was introduced in November 2001 when the S63 AMG with a tuned V12 engine replaced the S55 AMG. It was a short-lived model, however, because a new Mercedes V12 was in the offing.

That new engine came with twin turbochargers and replaced the old one in the S600 models as part of an extensive range overhaul in 2002. Engine changes were the primary focus, and an S55 Kompressor AMG introduced raw power where the earlier S63 AMG had been merely fast. In the mainstream range, a big-bore 3.7-litre petrol V6 created the S350, which replaced the S320, and a new OM648 diesel in the S320 CDI brought more power and torque. Yet the changes were unable to reverse a decline in sales that set in after 2001.

There were no major visual alterations, but a new grille and modified bumpers were added, along with redesigned tail lights and new alloy wheel styles. A new integrated suite of electronic safety measures called Pre-Safe became standard and 4Matic – extensively redesigned to improve reliability – became optional on some models. This was its first appearance on any S-Class, and had been prompted by the success in the USA of Quattro (four-wheel-drive) versions of the Audi A8 luxury saloons.

The final changes were made in the first half of 2003. An AMG V12 became available again in the S65 AMG, mainly intended for the USA and now with the twin-turbo engine. The V8 models took on seven-speed automatic gearboxes in the spring, and the range then continued unchanged until the summer of 2005, when the last of 484,683 examples were built. The best-selling W220 was the diesel S320 CDI – a result unthinkable in the days of earlier S-Class ranges.

MODELS: S280, S280 (LWB), S320, S320 (LWB), S320 CDI (OM613), S320 CDI LWB (OM613), S320 CDI (OM648), S320 CDI LWB (OM648), S350, S350 (LWB), S400 CDI, S400 CDI (LWB), S430, S430 (LWB), S500, S500 (LWB), S55 AMG, S55 AMG (LWB), S55 AMG Kompressor, S55 AMG Kompressor (LWB), S600 (M137), S600 (M275), S63 AMG, S65 AMG.

ENGINES: 2799cc M112 petrol V6 with 204 PS (S280 & S280 LWB); 3199cc M112 petrol V6 with 224 PS (S320 & S320 LWB); 3222cc OM613 diesel six with 197 PS (S320 CDI & S320 CDI LWB); 3222cc OM648 diesel six with 204 PS (S320 CDI & S320 CDI LWB); 3724cc M112 petrol V6 with 245 PS (S350 & S350 LWB); 3996cc OM628 diesel V8

The extended-wheelbase Pullman models could be had as either an S500 or S600.
This four-door configuration was standard.

with 250 PS (S400 CDI & S400 CDI LWB); 4266cc M113 petrol V8 with 279 PS (S430 & S430 LWB); 4966cc M113 petrol V8 with 306 PS (S500 & S500 LWB); 5439cc M113 petrol V8 with 360 PS (S55 AMG & S55 AMG LWB); 5439cc M113 supercharged V8 petrol with 500 PS (S55 AMG Kompressor & S55 AMG Kompressor LWB); 5513cc M275 twin-turbocharged petrol V12 with 500 PS (S600); 5786cc M137 petrol V12 with 367 PS (S600); 5980cc M275 twin-turbocharged petrol V12 with 600 PS (S65 AMG); 6258cc M137 petrol V12 with 444 PS (S63 AMG).

GEARBOXES: Five-speed automatic. Seven-speed automatic from spring 2003 (S430 and S500 only).

SUSPENSION, STEERING & BRAKES: Front suspension with four links, height-adjustable air springs, air-operated dampers and anti-roll bar. Rear suspension with five links, height-adjustable air springs, air-operated dampers and anti-roll bar. Rack-and-pinion steering with power assistance. Disc brakes all round, ventilated at the front; power assistance and ABS.

DIMENSIONS: Length: 5038mm or 5158mm (LWB models). **Width:** 1855mm. **Height:** 1444mm. **Wheelbase:** 2965mm or 3085mm (LWB models). **Track:** 1574mm (front and rear).

PERFORMANCE & FUEL CONSUMPTION: S280: 143mph, 24mpg, 0-100km/h in 9.7 sec; S320: 149mph, 22mpg, 0-100km/h in 8.2 sec; S320 CDI: 143mph, 28mpg, 0-100km/h in 8.8 sec; S350: 153mph, 23mpg, 0-100km/h in 7.6 sec; S400 CDI: 155mph, 26mpg, 0-100km/h in 7.8 sec; S430: 155mph (limited), 21mpg, 0-100km/h in 7.3 sec; S500: 155mph (limited), 19mpg, 0-100km/h in 6.5 sec; S55 AMG: 155mph (limited) or 174mph (unlimited), 18mpg, 0-100km/h in 6.0 sec; S55 AMG Kompressor: 155mph (limited) or 174mph (unlimited), 19mpg, 0-100km/h in 4.8 sec; S600: 155mph (limited), 18mpg, 0-100km/h in 6.3 sec; S65 AMG: 155mph (limited) or 186mph (unlimited), 16mpg, 0-100km/h in 4.5 sec.

PRODUCTION TOTALS: 484,683 (423,251 petrol and 61,446 diesel).

The W201 range, 1982-1993

Two main factors prompted Mercedes to introduce a 'compact' saloon range below their mainstream models in the early 1980s. One factor was market demand for smaller and more fuel-efficient cars in the wake of the two oil crises in the 1970s, and the other was the success of the BMW 3 series that met that demand very well. By the late 1970s, work was therefore under way to expand the Mercedes saloon range downwards with a completely new model. It was only ever intended to be a four-door saloon (despite experiments with other configurations) but there would eventually be a large diversity of model variants.

The car was developed under the internal designation W201 and designed to be physically smaller than existing mainstream saloons. Careful styling by Bruno Sacco also helped make it appear even smaller, and also brought an efficient aerodynamic look that nevertheless had a great deal of character and did not date in 11 years of production. The W201s were first with the single-arm 'jumping' wiper blade and also with the compact MacPherson strut front suspension

Visually closely related to the then unreleased W124 range, the W201 or 190 range took Mercedes into a new market sector.

Strongest seller was the 2-litre 190E saloon. Rectangular tail lights distinguished these cars readily from the larger 124 models.

The high-performance 190E 2.3-16 had deep flank protection panels, front and rear spoilers and, of course, alloy wheels.

The 190D 2.5 Turbo looked like any other W201 except for the air intake in its right-hand front wing.

and five-link rear suspension later shared with the W124 medium saloons.

Despite a major publicity fanfare, the range introduced in late 1982 was cautiously small, consisting only of a carburettor 190 and an injected 190E, both with developments of existing petrol engines. A year later came a 190D diesel model with a new noise encapsulation system and the option of a five-speed manual gearbox, while the cars were introduced to the USA with larger engines to overcome emissions requirements: the petrol model was a 190E with a 2.3-litre engine and the diesel a 190D with a long-stroke 2.2-litre size. Strong sales sanctioned the next step, already in preparation, which was a high-performance homologation special with a 16-valve engine developed by Cosworth in Britain and called the 190E 2.3-16. Later motorsport cars would evolve from this model, announced in September 1984. A new top diesel model then arrived in May 1985 with the five-cylinder diesel engine from the W124 250D and wearing 190D 2.5 badges.

Plans by the West German government to make catalytic converters mandatory on new cars led to the introduction of the first European 190s so equipped in September 1985, just two months before production of the half-millionth W201 made it clear that the 'compact' Mercedes had been a major

The six-cylinder 190E 2.6 expanded the range upwards. It was hard to recognise unless the tail badging was visible.

US models yet again had to have special headlamps. This is a post-face-lift six-cylinder model, with plastic flank panels.
(Mr.choppers, CC-by-SA 3.0)

Bright new colours were available on the 190E 2.5-16 that replaced the original 16-valve model.

success. From September 1986, cars were made either with catalytic converters or ready to receive them when they became mandatory.

This second phase of the range's production brought larger-engined models to broaden the W201's appeal. From April 1986, the 190E 2.6 came with the six-cylinder engine from the 260E to create a compact luxury model, while in the USA the five-cylinder diesel was turbocharged to create an automatic-only 190D 2.5 Turbo a few months later. That car was then made available outside the USA in September 1987, and in the meantime a 190E 2.3 went on sale in Europe from September 1986 (though not in Britain).

The millionth W201 was built in spring 1988, just a few months before the third phase of the range's existence was introduced by a major mid-life face-lift. The most obvious change for the 1989 models was the addition of plastic protection panels on the lower flanks (similar to those on the 190E 2.3-16); in theory, these matched the main body colour, but the matching process was imperfect and sometimes contrasting colours were used instead. Changes to the interior brought brighter colours, more leg room and two individual rear seats instead of a bench.

A highlight of the new range was a 190E 2.5-16, again a homologation special reflecting motorsport requirements, and over

the next two years there would be further-enhanced limited-edition models that allowed the W201s to remain competitive on the tracks. First was the 190E 2.5-16 Evolution in March 1989, followed a year later by the Evolution II, distinguished by spoilers and extended wheelarches that were quite outrageous on a road car.

Catalytic converters were standardised for all markets in September 1989, and at the same time the Sportline options, which included a lower ride height, were introduced. By this stage, the 190 with its carburettor engine was looking underpowered, so Mercedes replaced it in mid-1990 (later in some markets) with the 190E 1.8, which had a smaller-capacity injected derivative of the existing engine that actually delivered better performance. At the same time, the old 190E with its injected 2-litre engine was renamed a 190E 2.0.

The last phase of W201 production opened in March 1992 with a series of limited-run special editions that explored the market for a more youthful approach. The final specification changes, all minor, were then made in October 1992 and the last W201s were built in Germany in August 1993.

More than 1.8 million examples had been built by the time production came to an end in 1993. There had been just one CKD operation, in South Africa, but the W201

There was no mistaking this: the Evolution II limited-production model homologated features needed to keep the compact Mercedes competitive on the race tracks.

had also been cloned (if not very well) in North Korea. The range had attracted its own customising and tuning experts, and played a major part in changing public perceptions of the Mercedes marque during the 1980s and 1990s. So did the racing programme, and especially the works-supported teams in the DTM (German Touring Car Championship) that Klaus Ludwig won in 1992.

MODELS: 190, 190D, 190D 2.2, 190D 2.5, 190D 2.5 Turbo, 190E, 190E 1.8, 190E 2.0, 190E 2.3, 190E 2.3-16, 190E 2.5-16, 190E 2.5-16 Evolution I, 190E 2.5-16 Evolution II, 190E 2.6.

ENGINES: 1797cc M102 injected petrol four with 109PS (190E 1.8); 1997cc M102 petrol four with 90PS or (from October 1984) 105PS or 102PS with KAT (190); 1997cc M102 injected petrol four with 122PS or 118PS with KAT (190E & 190E 2.0); 1997cc OM601 diesel four with 72PS or 75PS from 1992 (190D); 2197cc OM601 diesel four with 73PS (190D 2.2); 2299cc M102 injected petrol four with 136PS, or 132PS with KAT, or 114PS, and later 132PS for USA (190E 2.3); 2299cc M102 injected petrol DOHC four with 185PS, or 170PS with KAT (190E 2.3-16); 2463cc M102 injected petrol DOHC four with 204PS, or 195PS with KAT (190E 2.5-16 Evolution I); 2463cc M102 injected petrol DOHC four with 235PS (190E 2.5-16 Evolution

II); 2497cc OM602 diesel five with 90PS, or 94PS from 1992 (190D 2.5); 2497cc OM602 turbocharged diesel five with 122PS, or 126PS from 1989 (190D 2.5 Turbo); 2498cc M102 injected petrol DOHC four with 204PS or 195PS with KAT (190E 2.5-16); 2599cc M103 injected petrol six with 166PS, or 160PS with KAT (190E 2.6).

GEARBOXES: Four-speed manual. Five-speed manual. Five-speed close-ratio manual (190E 2.3-16). Four-speed automatic.

SUSPENSION, STEERING & BRAKES: Front suspension with MacPherson struts, wishbones, coil springs, and anti-roll bar; hydropneumatic height adjustment optional on 190E 2.5-16 and standard on Evo I and Evo II. Rear suspension with five links, coil springs, and anti-roll bar; hydropneumatic self-levelling strut optional, and standard on 190E 2.3-16, 190E 2.5-16, Evo I and Evo II. Recirculating-ball steering; power assistance optional to 1985 (standard on 190E 2.3-16 and 190D 2.5) and standard from 1986. Disc brakes on all four wheels, ventilated at the front on 190E 2.3-16; dual hydraulic circuit and servo assistance; ABS optional (standard on 190E 2.3-16 from December 1984, standard on all US models from 1985, and standard on 190E 2.5-16, Evo I, Evo II, and 190E 2.6).

DIMENSIONS: Length: 4420mm; 4430mm for 190E 2.3-16 & 190E 2.5-16; 4448mm for US models from 1989. **Width:** 1678mm;

1706mm for 190E 2.3-16 & 190E 2.5-16; 1720mm for Evo I. **Height:** 1383mm; 1390mm from January 1985; 1375mm from 1989; 1353mm with Sportline option; 1361mm for 190E 2.3-16 & 190E 2.5-16; 1327-1372mm (adjustable) for Evo I and Evo II. **Wheelbase:** 2665mm. **Track:** 1428mm (front), 1437mm from January 1985, 1445mm for 190E 2.3-16 & 190E 2.5-16, 1452mm with Sportline option, 1478mm for Evo I & Evo II; 1415mm (rear), 1418mm from January 1985, 1421mm from 1989, 1429mm for 190E 2.3-16, 1431mm for 190E 2.5-16, 1432mm with Sportline option, 1453mm for Evo I & Evo II.

PERFORMANCE & FUEL CONSUMPTION:
190 112mph, 25mpg, 0-100km/h in 12.7 sec; 190D 99mph, 34mpg, 0-100km/h in 18.1 sec; 190D 2.2 99mph, 45mpg, 01-00km/h in 18.4 sec; 190D 2.5 108mph, 33mpg, 0-100km/h in 14.8 sec; 190D 2.5 Turbo 119mph, 29mpg, 0-100km/h in 11.5 sec; 190E 1.8 115mph, 27mpg, 0-100km/h in 12.3 sec; 190E/190E 2.0 121mph, 27mpg, 0-100km/h in 10.5 sec; 190E 2.3 121mph, 26mpg, 0-100km/h in 10.3 sec (without KAT); 190E 2.3-16 143mph, 28mpg, 0-100km/h in 8.2 sec (without KAT); 190E 2.5-16 143mph, 26mpg, 0-100km/h in 7.7 sec (with KAT); Evolution I 143mph, 26mpg, 0-100km/h in 7.7 sec (with KAT); Evolution II 155mph, 24mpg,

0-100km/h in 7.1 sec; 190E 2.6 130mph, 23mpg, 0-100km/h in 9.2 sec (with KAT).
PRODUCTION TOTALS: 190: 118,561; 190D: 452,806; 190D 2.2: 10,560; 190D 2.5: 147,502; 190D 2.5 Turbo 20,915; 190E 1.8: 173,354; 190E/190E 2.0 638,180; 190E 2.3: 186,610; 190E 2.3-16: 19,487; 190E 2.6: 104,907.

The W202 C-Class, 1993-2001

Mercedes' second compact saloon range was developed as the W202 but was known as a C-Class (for 'compact') when it entered production. It promised a wider engine range

The second-generation compact Mercedes had a much more rounded style that was more in keeping with its times. This is an early Elegance model.

The rising belt line of the W202 was more apparent from some angles than others.

Bright colours were intended to increase the W202's appeal to younger buyers. This early car has the Esprit trim level and alloy wheels.

than before, as well as better rear legroom, and was designed to draw younger customers into the Mercedes fold. Estate (S202) models were added to the saloons, and the basic platform was later used for the W208 CLK and R170 SLK models.

The styling anticipated the softer shapes of the 1990s with more rounded contours, as well as improved aerodynamics. However, a drive to reduce production costs was noticeable in less solid interior mouldings, which gave these cars a rather different character from their predecessors. A driver's airbag was made standard and a passenger's side bag optional, while belt tensioners were standard. A major change in marketing emphasis led to the creation of four trim levels, called Classic (added in 1995), Esprit, Elegance and Sport, the latter complemented by quicker steering.

On the engineering side, the five-link rear suspension of the W201s was retained, but a double-wishbone system at the front replaced the old cars' MacPherson struts. All-round disc brakes were designed with ABS as standard (onto which various traction control systems which would later be grafted).

All the W202 saloons in the autumn 1993 first release had multi-valve engines. The two petrol four-cylinders were the C180 and C220; these were accompanied by a four-cylinder C220 Diesel and a five-cylinder C250 Diesel. Only the 1.8-litre engine was really new, and the diesels both had oxidation catalysts and an EGR (Exhaust Gas Recirculation) system. For the USA, the only model in November

1993 was the C220, which did not have the four specification levels used elsewhere.

A six-cylinder C280 (also sold in the USA), along with entry-level C200 petrol and C200 diesel types expanded the range in early 1994; the diesel became the only two-valve engine in the range. These were followed in June by the first performance model, the C36 AMG with the enlarged M104 six-cylinder engine. Unsurprisingly, this also became available in the USA.

The half-millionth W202 was built in February 1995, and that September the C230 Kompressor introduced supercharger technology to the range. From May 1996 the estates finally went on sale, although not in the USA. They could be bought with most of the existing engines.

The whole range had its mid-life face-lift in June 1997, visual changes being redesigned front and rear aprons, body-colour sills, smoked indicator lenses in the tail-lights and a new selection of alloy wheel styles. Interior trims and some of the switchgear also changed, while a service interval indicator and an electronic key fob became standard. The first V6 petrol engines also became available, three-valve all-aluminium M112 types that created C240 and C280 models. At the top of the range, the new 306PS V8 C43 AMG replaced the straight-six C36 AMG and was built on the lines at Stuttgart rather than at the AMG premises.

In 1998, it was the turn of the diesel range to get new models, which were the first 202 models with common-rail engines.

A single 2151cc capacity four-cylinder had different electronic control units to deliver outputs appropriate to the C200 CDI and the C220 CDI. At the other end of the range, a C55 AMG replaced the C43 AMG in June 1998, but these cars were built to order in tiny numbers. The last significant modification for the 202 range was standardisation of the ESP stability control system during the 1999 season.

Saloon production ended in September 2000, but the estates continued until May 2001. Despite some quality control issues, the 202 range had been another big success for Mercedes, and overtook the E-Class to become the marque's best-seller for most of its production life. Close to 1.9 million examples were built, saloon production vastly outstripping that of estates, and in 1998, its best single year, almost 320,000 examples left the assembly lines.

MODELS: Saloon: C180, C200, C200CDI, C200 Diesel, C200 Kompressor, C220, C220 Biodiesel, C220 CDI, C220 Diesel, C230, C230 Kompressor, C240, C250 Diesel, C250 Turbodiesel, C280 (M104), C280 (M112), C36 AMG, C43 AMG, C55 AMG. **Estate:** C180, C200, C200 CDI, C200 Diesel, C200 Kompressor, C220 CDI, C220 Diesel, C230, C230 Kompressor, C240, C250 Turbodiesel, C280 (M112), C43 AMG, C55 AMG.

ENGINES: 1799cc M111 petrol four with 122 PS (C180). 1997cc OM601 diesel four with 75 PS or (from 1996) 88PS (C200 Diesel). 1998cc M111 petrol four with 136 PS (C200). 1998cc M111 supercharged petrol four with 184 PS or (from 1996) 192PS. (C200 Kompressor). 2148cc OM611 diesel four with 102PS (C200 CDI). 2148cc OM611 diesel four with 125PS (C220 CDI). 2151cc OM611 diesel four with 102 PS (C200 CDI). 2151cc OM611 diesel four with 125 PS (C220 CDI). 2155cc OM604 diesel four with 95 PS (C220 Diesel). Also available as 75PS Biodiesel engine. 2199cc M111 petrol four with 150 PS (C220). 2295cc M111 petrol four with 150PS (C230). 2295cc M111 supercharged petrol four with 193 PS (C230 Kompressor). 2398cc M112 petrol V6 with 170 PS (C240). 2497cc OM605 diesel five with 113 PS (C250 Diesel). 2497cc OM605 turbocharged diesel five with 150 PS (C250 Turbodiesel). 2799cc M104 petrol six with 193 PS (C280). 2799cc M112 petrol V6 with 197 PS (C280). 3606cc M104 petrol six with 280 PS (C36 AMG). 4266cc M113 petrol

The estate models were really lifestyle cars, with only modest load capacity. This is a 220CDI variant.

More variations on a theme: the wheels on this estate mark it out as a Sport variant.

V8 with 306 PS (C43 AMG). 5439cc M113 petrol V8 with 347 PS (C55 AMG).
GEARBOXES: Five-speed manual (not available on AMG Cars). Four-speed automatic (to 1996). Five-speed automatic (from 1996)
SUSPENSION, STEERING & BRAKES: Front suspension with twin unequal-length wishbones, coil springs, gas dampers and anti-roll bar. Rear suspension with five links, coil springs, gas dampers and anti-roll bar (no rear anti-roll bar on C180 or C200 Diesel). Recirculating-ball steering with power assistance. Disc brakes all round, ventilated at the front on some models and at the rear on C43 AMG and C55 AMG; servo assistance and ABS.

DIMENSIONS: Length: 4487mm. **Width:** 1720mm. **Height:** 1418mm. **Wheelbase:** 2690mm. **Track:** 1499mm later 1505mm (front), 1465mm (rear).
PERFORMANCE & FUEL CONSUMPTION: Figures are for saloon variants with manual gearbox unless otherwise indicated. Estate models are typically slightly slower and slightly thirstier.
C200 Diesel 99mph, 37mpg, 0-100km/h in 19.6 sec; C220 Diesel 109mph, 33mpg, 0-100km/h in 16.3 sec; C220 CDI 123mph, 46mpg, 0-100km/h in 10.5 sec; C250 Diesel 116mph, 38mpg, 0-100km/h in 15.3 sec (auto); C180: 120mph, 26mpg, 0-100km/h in 12 sec; C200 Kompressor 140mph, 23mpg, 0-100km/h in 8.8 sec; C230: 130mph, 26mpg, 0-100km/h in 10.5 sec; C230 Kompressor 143mph, 27mpg, 0-100km/h in 8.4 sec; C240: 133mph, 24mpg, 0-100km/h in 9.9 sec (auto); C280 (M112) 142mph, 25mpg, 0-100km/h in 8.5 sec (auto); C36 AMG 155mph (limited), 20mpg, 0-100km/h in 6.7 sec; C43 AMG 155mph (limited), 21.5mpg, 0-100km/h in 21.5 sec; C55 AMG 155mph (limited), 22.5mpg, 0-100km/h in 5.5 sec.
PRODUCTION TOTALS: 1,626,383 saloons; 243,871 estates.

This face-lift model S202 estate has the plastic wheel covers associated with the Esprit trim level. (M93, CC-by-SA 3.0)

The 300SL, 1954-1963

The legendary 300SL Gullwing coupé was born out of Mercedes' desire to get back into racing in the early 1950s. Still in postwar recovery mode, the company had to keep an eye on costs and therefore chose not to develop a Grand Prix car but rather a sports-racer that could use existing production components.

The 300SL coupé had its origins in pure racing models like this one.

The obvious engine choice was the latest 3-litre, and to compensate for its great weight the body would have to be very light. So the choice fell on a welded tubular space-frame with alloy panels and an aerodynamic shape; the tall engine was canted over by 40 degrees to give a low bonnet line. (Later, this would make RHD derivatives impossible.)

Open versions of the racers were built and were ultimately an inspiration for the 300SL roadster.

Both open and closed versions raced during 1952 with some success, and Mercedes' US agent, Max Hoffmann, suggested that a production version would sell well in the USA. When he promised an order for 1000, Stuttgart agreed to go ahead.

The new W198 model was based on a 1953 coupé version of the racer that had not actually competed, but was more consciously styled than the earlier cars. The coupé body gave better rigidity than the open type and also allowed a better-appointed interior. The space-frame made standard doors impossible and so half-depth doors were hinged from the roof and made to open upwards. This highly

The road-going 300SL coupé was a considerably more refined car, but still with much of the rawness of the racers.

The defining feature of the coupé was its 'gullwing' doors, which are fully displayed here.

This car is sporting the centre-lock wheels that were favoured for competition use.

The roadster version was made in response to calls for an open car from the USA.

distinctive feature – Flügeltür or wing-door in German but Gullwing in English – added an exotic appeal of its own even though access to the two-seat cabin was tricky. The steering wheel had to be hinged to help and, as there was no room for the windows to wind down, they were made removable. A new wide grille was, meanwhile, a visual success.

The first production prototype was ready by January 1954 and was displayed at the New York Show the following month. Production began in August 1954, and the cars were hand-built to order on a slow-moving assembly line. Over the next three years, just 1400 would be made.

The racers had been all-aluminium, but the production cars had steel bodies with aluminium doors, bonnet and boot lid. A lightweight all-aluminium version was offered from 1956, but only 29 were made. Standard cars had bolt-on steel wheels with conventional Mercedes hubcaps, but it was possible to order centre-lock types like the racers had.

The 3-litre iron-block engine was a special version with a dry sump lubrication system not seen on the racers, but a 300 saloon camshaft for everyday driveability. Its most exotic feature was the fuel-injection system that was at the forefront of car technology in the 1950s. Gearbox, transmission components, and the recirculating-ball steering all came from the saloon, and so did the double-pivot swing-axle rear end, which could give alarming handling in such a fast car. Actual speeds depended on the specification and the axle ratio chosen, but typically a Gullwing could reach 155-160mph. Such performance demanded good brakes, and Mercedes specified finned alloy Alfin drums all round, with a servo as standard.

Even though the Gullwing was a flawed design that needed better handling and brakes, it proved a sensation at the time. Today, more than seven decades after its introduction, it is still deservedly a thing of wonder.

The Gullwing was a big success in the USA, as Max Hoffmann had predicted. Nevertheless, it was clear that there would also be a market for an open model, especially in California. Mercedes therefore decided to create such a car and to address some of the Gullwing's shortcomings at the same time. The result was the 300SL Roadster, which was introduced in 1957 and replaced the Gullwing on the assembly lines.

The modified space-frame chassis was under development by summer 1956. It had shallower sills to allow deeper doors, and a longer tail to provide decent luggage space. The front end panels were reworked with the vertical light clusters planned for the Fintail saloons (although a halogen option for the USA required modified versions), and the handling was improved by the latest single-pivot swing-axle design pioneered on the 220 and further tamed by a horizontal spring that reduced roll.

Winding windows, a folding soft top, and space-frame reinforcements added to the new roadster's weight, and to maintain performance the engine was uprated with a new camshaft. A selection of axle ratios allowed the car to be specified as a fast boulevard cruiser or a hard sports-racer, with a variety of options in between. There were

A comparison of this car with the racing roadster reveals where the space-frame had been altered to allow for deeper doors.

changes to the dashboard, the steering wheel was now fixed, and the handbrake lever now lived between the seats. The only glaring omission when the roadster was previewed at the 1957 Geneva Show was any improvement to the brakes, although the smaller fuel tank made necessary by the larger boot was hardly a step in the right direction.

Volume production began in May 1957 and lasted until 1963. From September 1958 it was possible to buy a sleek removable hardtop, or even to buy the roadster as a coupé with the same hardtop fixed in place. All-round disc brakes were long overdue when they finally arrived in March 1961, and the last 229 cars had an all-alloy engine, similar to that introduced in 1961 for the Fintail 300SE saloons but of course in a much higher state of tune.

A build total of 1858 examples made the 300SL Roadster more numerous than its Gullwing predecessor, but in fact it sold more slowly over the six years of its production. Its more sybaritic approach also hinted at the way Mercedes would go in the future with its sports models.

MODELS: 300SL Gullwing coupé, 300SL Roadster.
ENGINE: 2996cc M198 injected petrol six with 195PS or 215PS.
GEARBOX: Four-speed manual.
SUSPENSION, STEERING & BRAKES: Front suspension with wishbones, coil springs and anti-roll bar. Rear suspension with swing axles and coil springs; roadsters with single-pivot swing-axle and compensating spring. Recirculating-ball steering, unassisted. Drum brakes all round to March 1961; disc brakes on front wheels from March 1961; power assistance standard.
DIMENSIONS: Length: 4530 mm (Coupé); 4570mm (Roadster). **Width:** 1790mm. **Height:** 1300mm. **Wheelbase:** 2400mm. **Track:** 1385mm (front), 1435mm (rear) Coupé; 1398mm (front), 1448mm (rear) Roadster.
PERFORMANCE & FUEL CONSUMPTION: Coupé: 146-161mph, 17mpg, 0-100km/h in 10 sec; Roadster: 137-155mph, 17mpg, 0-100km/h in 10 sec.
PRODUCTION TOTALS: Coupé: 1400; Roadster: 1858.

The 190SL, 1955-1962

When Max Hoffmann proposed a production version of the racing 300SL to the Mercedes Board, he also pointed out that such an expensive car would need to be accompanied by a more affordable open two-seater model at much lower cost. The Board agreed, and set its engineers to work on the W121 project, facing a deadline of just five months before it was to be launched alongside the 300SL at the New York Show in February 1954.

Obviously, the only option was to draw on existing mechanical hardware, and the W121 was based on a shortened Ponton saloon floorpan. New elements already under development were added to the mix, including low-pivot swing-axle rear suspension and a 1.9-litre four-cylinder version of the existing OHC six-cylinder engine. This was suitably uprated with twin carburettors and the car was given Alfin finned alloy brake drums like those of the 300SL, with the option of a servo. As for styling, the car had to have a strong resemblance to the 300SL Gullwing coupé, and its steel body was visually based on the open 300SL that had raced in 1952.

Not everything had been settled by the time of the 1954 New York Show, but the prototype presented as a 190SL was

The 190SL was the 300SL's younger sibling, its focus more on touring comfort than on outright performance.

With its soft top erect, the 190SL presented a neat and sophisticated profile.

both credible and exciting. It came with the promise of a stripped-out club racer option with features such as alloy panels and aero screens, but enthusiastic customers for both

The 190SL of course had a realistically-sized boot, which the 300SL Gullwing did not.

The coupé version of the 190SL had a neat hardtop, which was sometimes painted to contrast with the main body.

Early versions of the coupé roof had a small rear window, as seen here.

standard and competition versions had to wait another year before the production cars were ready – and they incorporated several changes for the better. The production-specification 190SL was displayed at the Geneva Show in March 1955 and volume production began in May. This time, there would be RHD variants as well as the expected LHD types because Mercedes planned to make the 190SL a global model.

This was never intended as a car to rival the agile but spartan sports models from Britain. Mercedes saw it as a comfortable sports tourer, although rather confusingly called it a roadster. Two seats were standard, although a third sideways-facing seat could be had as an option. A top speed of around 110mph was very respectable, although that became rather optimistic soon after production began, when a lower axle ratio was standardised to improve acceleration. The promised competition version was put on sale but did not prove very popular, perhaps because of the 190SL's boulevard cruiser

image. It was therefore dropped after about a year.

The options were widened at the Frankfurt Show in November 1955, when a removable alloy hardtop option became available. This was fixed in place for the new coupé model, and buyers could also buy a car which had both soft top and removable hardtop. A further round of changes in spring 1956 brought additional bright trim and larger tail lights, while the hardtop changed to steel and there were more heavily padded seats and other equipment changes to meet buyer demand for luxury. Minor changes continued during 1957 and 1958.

Sales had started well, and 3000 cars were made by March 1956. However, sales began to slide in 1957, and the 190SL did not receive a shot in the arm until the start of the 1960 season, when a larger rear window in the soft top and a more stylish hardtop with wraparound rear window from the pen of Paul Bracq gave the car a more modern appearance. The sales boost was brief, though, and the downward trend began again.

Few changes were made in the cars' final years, perhaps the most obvious occurring during 1961 when different wheels with fewer ventilating slots became standard. Production for Europe was brought to an end in spring 1962, although new cars were still being made for the 190SL's best market of the USA until the end of the year. Production had actually finished by the time a formal last-of-line ceremony was held in February 1963, timed to coincide with the end of 300SL production.

Of 25,881 cars built in just under seven years, around 18,000 – or more than 70% – were sold in the USA. By modern standards, these figures are not large, but there is no doubt that the 190SL played a major role in establishing the Mercedes presence and image in the US market during the 1950s and early 1960s.

MODELS: 190SL Roadster (with optional hardtop), 190SL Coupé.
ENGINE: 1897cc M121 petrol four with 105PS.
GEARBOX: Four-speed manual.
SUSPENSION, STEERING & BRAKES:
Front suspension with twin wishbones, coil

springs and anti-roll bar. Rear suspension with low-pivot swing-axles and coil springs. Recirculating-ball steering. Drum brakes on all four wheels; power assistance initially optional, then standard from May 1956.
DIMENSIONS: Length: 4290mm. **Width:** 1740mm. **Height:** 1320mm. **Wheelbase:** 2400mm. **Track:** 1430mm (front), 1475mm (rear).
PERFORMANCE & FUEL CONSUMPTION: All models: 106mph, 23mpg, 0-100km/h in 14.5 sec.
PRODUCTION TOTAL: 25,881 (all models).

The later wraparound rear window gave the cars a more modern appearance.

The Pagodas, 1963-1971

The W113 'Pagoda' models definitively established the form of the Mercedes sports car. Produced as three successive models – 230SL, 250SL and 280SL – they combined high levels of comfort for two people with decent sporting performance and handling. Not only did they have to take over from the 190SL but they also had to fill a gap in the market left by the demise of the 300SL. Arguably, they failed to do so, but that did not prevent them from becoming a big sales success.

Mercedes had looked at the idea of a six-cylinder 220SL to overcome the performance deficiencies of the 190SL from 1957, but delays led to a rethink in 1960, and, by that time, new hardware was available to add to the specification. A new 300SL was ruled out (even though the latest alloy version of the

The Pagoda models focused on sophistication rather than performance, but were still quick machines in their day. This is a 230SL. (Lothar Spurzem, CC-by-SA 2.0)

3-litre engine was becoming available) and work focused on a smaller six-cylinder engine. A bored-out 220SE engine was already under development, and this was adopted, giving the new model the name of 230SL. It had 150bhp,

A neat and close-fitting soft top was expected of a Mercedes SL, and the Pagoda models delivered.

The coupé roof could be painted to contrast with the body, as on the 190SL. Its 'pagoda' shape was more clearly visible from in front or behind the car.

bigger valves and an improved injection system, and proved capable of giving the finished car a 120mph top speed.

Just as the 190SL had added a new body to a shortened saloon platform, so the new W113 model added a new body to a shortened Fintail saloon platform. Bonnet, boot lid,

door skins and tonneau cover were made of alloy to save weight, and the basic structure incorporated Mercedes' passenger safety cell with crumple zones front and rear. The boot was planned from the start to be generously sized.

The new body was a Paul Bracq design which combined fashionable Italianate lines with the wide 'sports' grille of the earlier SLs, and vertical front light stacks matching those on the top-model Fintails. Yet its defining feature was the removable hardtop, with deep side windows and raised edges alongside a recessed centre. The shape reminded onlookers of a Chinese pagoda roof, and from that resemblance came the lasting nickname of Pagoda.

There were no pure coupé models, but only a roadster (with soft top and winding windows) or a roadster with detachable hardtop. The interior was for two only, but a sideways-facing third seat was optional. Cabin trim was designed to minimise protrusions; the dash was

The dip in the centre of the roof can be seen in this picture, which shows off the car's sleek lines.

There was a clear family resemblance between the W113 and other Mercedes models designed by Paul Bracq.

padded and did not have the wood of the Fintail two-door type that was its inspiration.

Much of the running-gear was shared with the Fintail models. The W113 had the more direct recirculating-ball steering of the two-door types, with optional power assistance. It combined front disc brakes with Alfin rear drums of the type used on earlier SLs, plus a servo and twin hydraulic circuits. A 14in wheel size was chosen (larger than the Fintails) and new tyres had to be specially designed to suit. With the low-pivot swing axles and horizontal compensating spring at the rear, handling was good if not overtly sporting. However, the manual gearbox was a compromise based on an existing type and its ratios were not ideal. The four-speed Mercedes-built fluid-coupled automatic option proved more popular.

The 230SL was no performance model, but that did not stop Mercedes from entering examples in the works-sponsored competition teams. They were successful, too: in 1963, Eugen Böhringer won the Spa-Sofia Liège endurance rally in a lightweight 230SL, and the following year finished third in a special car running a non-production 2.6-litre engine. In 1965, Dieter Glemser claimed third place in the Acropolis rally with a works-prepared lightweight 230SL.

There were few changes to the 230SL in its three years of production, though a larger fuel tank was fitted from October 1964. Generally, the styling was well regarded, and when Pininfarina built a sleek 230SL coupé in 1964, there was no call for more. Frua tried its hand

with a '230SLX' shooting-brake in 1966 but again the car remained unique.

The new seven-bearing 2.5-litre engine introduced for top-model saloons in autumn 1965 was a natural choice for the second-stage W113. Production of the 230SL ended in January 1967, and the new 250SL was introduced at the Geneva Show in March. It offered the same 150bhp as the earlier car, but a useful torque increase made it well suited to the four-speed automatic gearbox that remained the favourite choice.

The 250SL came with all-round disc brakes and full-size wheel trims – and of course had gained weight. A choice of axle ratios enabled buyers to emphasise acceleration or high-speed cruising. Further changes for the 1968 season mainly affected the interior and focused on its safety features. Meanwhile, the USA was briefly offered a 'California Coupé' variant, which came with the removable hardtop while the hood well was repurposed to provide a fully upholstered fold-down bench seat suitable only for children.

This second iteration of the W113 lasted in production for only just over a year. The new 2.8-litre six-cylinder engine introduced in top-model saloons in autumn 1967 reached the sports cars in December 1967 with 160PS, improving both peak power and torque delivery. The new 280SL nevertheless needed a lower axle ratio to maintain performance in the face of increased weight, so the engine had to rev harder than its predecessors.

Other 280SL changes reflected customer demands. Softer springs and dampers

produced more body roll, while rubber joints in the suspension, designed to reduce maintenance, made the handling less crisp. Then from later in 1968, US cars lost 10PS as their engines were adjusted to

American lighting regulations called for special headlights and side marker lights on later models. This one is a 1971 280SL. (Andrew Bone, CC-by-SA 2.0)

meet new emissions control regulations. The revised engines needed a new cooling system, too, which subsequently became standard on all 280SL models. For 1969, US models also required special headlamps. Fuchs 'Mexican hat' alloy wheels became optional in August 1970, and the last 280SL was built in March 1971.

Of nearly 49,000 W113 cars built, about 40% were sold in the USA. The attraction for US customers increased over time: under 25% of 230SLs crossed the Atlantic; more than 33% of 250SLs followed, and more than 50% of 280SLs found owners in the USA. By far the best seller, both in terms of overall numbers and of annual averages, was the 280SL – which made clear that Mercedes had got the SL formula right by the time that model went on sale.

MODELS: 230SL, 250SL, 280SL.
ENGINES: 2281cc M127 injected petrol six with 150PS (230SL); 2496cc M129 injected petrol six with 150PS (250SL); 2778cc M130 injected petrol six with 170PS (280SL).
GEARBOX: Four-speed manual. Four-speed automatic. Five-speed manual (option, from January 1966). Five-speed overdrive manual (US option, from September 1969).
SUSPENSION, STEERING & BRAKES: Front suspension with wishbones, coil springs and anti-roll bar. Rear suspension with single-pivot swing axle, compensating spring and coil springs. Recirculating-ball steering with optional power assistance. Disc brakes on front wheels and drum on the rears; power assistance standard.
DIMENSIONS: Length: 4285mm. **Width:** 1760mm. **Height:** 1305mm; 1320mm with soft top erect. **Wheelbase:** 2400mm. **Track:** 1485mm (front), 1485mm (rear).
PERFORMANCE & FUEL CONSUMPTION: 230SL manual: 124mph, 19mpg, 0-100km/h in 11 sec; 230SL auto: 121mph, 17.5mpg, 0-100km/h in 11 sec; 250SL manual: 121mph, 17.5mpg, 0-100km/h in 12 sec; 250SL auto: 118mph, 17mpg, 0-100km/h in 12 sec; 280SL manual: 124mph, 17mpg, 0-100km/h in 11 sec; 280SL auto: 121mph, 16mpg, 0-100km/h in 11 sec.
PRODUCTION TOTALS: 230SL: 19,831; 250SL: 5196; 280SL: 23,885.

The R107 SL, 1971-1989

Like their W113 Pagoda predecessors, the R107 SL models went through three major stages or generations, although their 18-year production run was more than twice as long as the eight-year life of the W113s. The factory code of R107 appears not to have been applied at the start of production, but entered use later on; the R prefix stood for roadster.

These two-seater sports models were designed at a time when the US market – where success was crucial – was demanding increased passive-safety measures. Mercedes had its own very high safety standards, but engineered the cars to exceed the US standards so that there would be less need for major re-engineering to meet any stricter standards in the future. Inevitably, this added weight, and it also led to the cars' German nickname of Panzerwagen, which means tank or armoured car. The strength of the bodyshell was not visibly obvious, except perhaps in the sturdy windscreen pillars that had been designed to resist a rollover. The detachable steel hardtop option was as heavy as ever, and the all-steel bodyshells were galvanised to resist corrosion.

The extra weight called for more powerful engines, and although an uprated twin-cam 2.8-litre engine was planned from the start for some countries, the new 280SL was held over. The primary engine at launch in 1971 was Mercedes' latest 3.5-litre cast iron V8 – although there was a 4.5-litre engine for US models to overcome the losses from emissions control gear. Much of the running-gear came from the Stroke 8 saloons, which were still

The R107 models previewed the styling that would be seen on the W116 S Class saloons. This is an early 350SL.

American regulations still required special lighting features, and now extended bumpers, too.

relatively new at the time. So there were twin wishbones at the front and semi-trailing arms at the rear, with coil springs all round. Both front and rear anti-roll bars were standard; power-assisted steering was also standard and the brakes were discs all round (ventilated at the front) with servo assistance and twin hydraulic circuits.

The new 107 models had the same overall size and layout as the W113s they replaced, but the styling employed several visual tricks. Rectangular headlamps flanking the horizontal grille made the cars look wider and more solid. The gentle wedge shape, meanwhile, had blacked-out sills to reduce the visual height, while side rubbing-strips made the cars look longer. Early on in development, the decision had been made that the replacement for the big Fintail-based coupé models should be a long-wheelbase derivative of the 107 programme (see p85), and some styling decisions inevitably reflected the need for the two models to share visual cues.

The instruments were clearly arranged in a cowled binnacle, and there was a large four-spoke steering wheel. A centre console between the seats carried the

handbrake on RHD cars, but LHD models had a foot-operated parking brake. Built-in air-conditioning was among the options, as was a cramped rear bench seat that was little more than a token. Inertia-reel belts and head restraints were made standard soon after the cars were introduced.

The first-generation cars were introduced in April 1971 with the name of 350SL and a choice between four-speed manual and four-speed fluid flywheel automatic gearboxes. Either standard steel wheels or Fuchs alloy types could be ordered. For the USA, however, the car introduced in July 1971 with the 350SL name actually had a 4.5-litre engine and slightly less power, thanks to its emissions control specification. Later cars to the stricter Californian regulations lost even more power. The 4.5-litre engine came only with a three-speed torque-converter automatic, and this gearbox was standardised on the 350SL as well in summer 1972. US models came with twin round headlamps, running lights in place of the front turn indicators and turn signal lamps let into the front bumpers, which were extended in 1974 to meet new low-speed impact legislation.

With the 500SL came a discreet tail spoiler. This example is wearing the Fuchs alloy wheels that were optional on other models.

The 500SL typically had dark lower panels as a distinguishing feature. The ribbed tail light lenses were a Mercedes characteristic of the period.

An unrestricted 4.5-litre engine became available outside the USA from March 1973 in a 450SL model alongside the 350SL, and this soon became the best-seller. The emissions-controlled US car was renamed a 450SL, but the autumn 1973 oil crisis now led to a drop in global sales. Mercedes responded by adding the planned six-cylinder 280SL to the range in autumn 1974, but not in the UK or the USA. There was revised gearing for the manual-gearbox cars and a five-speed overdrive gearbox became available as well.

There were several minor specification changes in the later 1970s, and the requirement for catalytic converters on the US 450SL for 1979 ruined that model's performance. Nevertheless, these three first-generation models – 280SL, 350SL and 450SL – remained available into 1980. The 350SL went out of production in March, but the 450SL lasted until November, primarily to meet US demand. The 280SL, meanwhile, carried on into the next phase of the 107's existence.

The second-generation cars were mainly distinguished by new engines, and were in production from 1980 to 1985. They consisted of 280SL, 380SL and 500SL models. The 380SL and 500SL both came with new fuel-efficient light-alloy V8s, of 3.8 litres and 5.0 litres respectively. The 500SL had alloy wheels and a tail spoiler as standard, and ABS was an option on all models. Both hard and soft tops were now supplied with all cars, and four-speed torque-converter automatics became available on all three models.

Once again there was a special model for the USA, where the 3.8-litre V8 had different bore and stroke dimensions for better emissions efficiency. Then, in autumn 1981, the US dimensions were standardised for all engines as part of Mercedes' Energy Concept fuel-saving revisions programme. All engines lost some power but top speeds were maintained thanks to taller gearing, and on the 280SL the five-speed manual gearbox became standard.

The third-generation cars were introduced at the Frankfurt Show in 1985, and were visually cleaner than earlier models, with 15in flush-faced alloy wheels (which allowed larger brake discs), flush-fitting door handles, and a new chin spoiler. The face-lift affected the interior, too, with recontoured seats and a more comprehensive instrument panel. Only the 500SL engine was carried over; a new 300SL with the latest 3-litre straight-six replaced the 280SL, while an enlarged 420SL replaced the 380SL. To restore performance lost to emissions control changes on the 500SL, there was a new top-model 560SL for non-European markets. All these engines came with a new computer-controlled Bosch injection system and all except the 5.6-litre V8 were built in either KAT (catalyst-equipped) or RüF (catalyst-ready) form in preparation for new emissions requirements in West Germany. Catalysts became standard there in 1986.

These third-generation models were highly successful, despite the age of the basic design, and the 107 range had its best-ever sales season in 1986. The bigger-engined cars were the best-sellers, as usual, and the last 107 models were built in summer 1989.

The mid-life face-lift brought a lighter look, with new flat-faced alloy wheels, too.

MODELS: 280SL, 300SL, 350SL, 350SL 4.5, 380SL, 420SL, 450SL, 500SL, 560SL.
ENGINES: 2746cc M110 DOHC petrol six with 185PS (280SL); 2962cc M103 petrol six with 190PS (300SL); 3499cc M116 petrol V8 with 200PS (350SL); 3818cc M116 petrol V8 with 218PS (380SL to 1981); 3839cc M116 petrol V8 with 204PS (380SL from 1981); 4196cc M116 petrol V8 with 218PS (420SL); 4520cc M117 petrol V8 with 225PS (450SL); 4973cc M117 petrol V8 with 245PS (500SL); 5547cc M117 petrol V8 with 242PS (560SL to 1987); 5547cc M117 petrol V8 with 300PS (560SL from 1987).
GEARBOX: Four-speed manual. Five-speed manual (280SL option). Three-speed automatic (450SL). Four-speed automatic.
SUSPENSION, STEERING & BRAKES: Front suspension with wishbones, coil springs and anti-roll bar. Rear suspension with semi-trailing arms, coil springs and anti-roll bar; hydraulic self-levelling optional from July 1972. Recirculating-ball steering with power assistance. Disc brakes all round with power assistance.
DIMENSIONS: Length: 4390mm; US models 4630mm to mid-1983 and then 4580mm. **Width:** 1790mm. **Height:** 1300mm; 1295mm with hardtop, 1305mm with soft top; 1297mm/1397mm for 300SL and 500SL from 1985; 1200/1300mm for 560SL. **Wheelbase:** 2460mm; 2455mm from 1985, except 2460mm for 300SL. **Track:** 1452mm (front), 1440mm (rear) to 1985; 1465mm (front), 1465mm (rear) from 1985.
PERFORMANCE & FUEL CONSUMPTION: 280SL manual: 128mph, 18mpg, 0-100km/h in 9.5 sec; 280SL auto: 128mph, 17.5mpg, 0-100km/h in 10.5 sec; 300SL: 123mph (121mph with KAT), 20mpg, 0-100km/h in 9.4 sec (9.8 sec with KAT); 350SL manual: 132mph, 15mpg, 0-100km/h in 9 sec; 350SL auto: 132mph, 15mpg, 0-100km/h in 10 sec; 380SL: 133mph (127mph with 204PS), 16.5mpg, 0-100km/h in 9.5 sec; 420SL: 132mph (127mph with KAT), 16mpg, 0-100km/h in 8.5 sec (9 sec with KAT); 450SL: 135mph, 15mpg, 0-100km/h in 9.5 sec; 500SL: 140mph (133mph with KAT) or 137mph with 213PS engine, 16.5mpg, 0-100km/h in 8.5 sec (to 1985), 7.3 sec (from 1985), 7.8 sec with KAT; 560SL: 138mph, 17mpg, 0-100km/h in 7.7 sec.
PRODUCTION TOTALS: 280SL: 25,436; 300SL: 13,742; 350SL: 15,304; 380SL: 53,200; 420SL: 2148; 450SL: 66,298; 500SL: 11,812; 560SL: 49,347.

This US-model 560SL shows the neat hardtop in place, along with the ugly third brakelight required in that country on the later cars.

The R129 SL, 1989-2001

The wedge-shaped body of the R129 SL is very clear in this picture of an early example.

The removable hardtop was a particularly successful piece of design. This is an early UK-registered car.

The soft top was another excellent piece of design, with superb fit and finish.

For the next generation of the SL sports models, the R129 types, Bruno Sacco's team designed a distinct wedge shape with a steeply raked windscreen and short tail. A sports grille was expected, and so were Sacco's favoured flank protection panels and a removable hardtop – though this was now made of alloy and standard rather than optional. The soft top was given power operation as standard, but an unexpected new feature was a rollover bar that was normally concealed within the bodywork behind the seats, but would pop up in under a second to provide occupant protection if sensors detected an imminent rollover.

In other respects, this was the familiar SL formula of a two-seat luxury roadster, now on a slightly longer wheelbase and an inch wider to provide more interior room, and still optionally available with impractical rear seats. New was a five-dial variant of the established three-dial instrument panel, and power-adjusted seats with a memory could be had on request. As in earlier SLs, the mechanical components were drawn from the mainstream ranges, and the R129 therefore had the same strut front and five-link rear suspension as its W201 and W124 contemporaries. The latest traction aids of ASR wheelspin control and the ASD limited-slip differential became optional, as did ADS damper control.

Sales began in autumn 1989 after a launch at the Geneva show and the R129 would go through three major phases. The USA

The low stance and special alloy wheels (with wider tyres at the rear) hint at the performance available from this SL60 AMG.

had been the primary market for the R107 models, and would become so again. The first cars were the six-cylinder 300SL and 300SL-24, and the V8-engined 500SL; in the USA, however, the base 300SL was not sold and the 24-valve car was badged as a plain 300SL.

Waiting lists quickly built up, and the range was then expanded to four models in summer 1992 with the addition of a V12-engined 600SL – with a deeper front bumper to maintain crash performance with the longer engine. In late summer 1993, the two 300 models were replaced by six-cylinder 280 and 320 types, and under the new naming convention the SL letters now became a prefix. So the four-model range for the 1994 and 1995 model years was badged as SL280, SL320, SL500 and SL600.

The second phase of R129 production was really transitional, and brought a continuous evolution for the 1996, 1997 and 1998 model years while the model range remained unchanged (although there were new AMG types; see below). First came a minor face-lift in mid-1995, with alterations to the wings' air vents and the introduction of side airbags, while five-speed automatics replaced the earlier type. The 1997 models then brought new wheel options, an automatic rain sensor, and the option of an expensive Panorama hardtop with a glass roof panel. This was the last season for the SL320 in the USA, which was withdrawn for 1998.

The third phase began with more cosmetic changes in 1998, notably body-coloured door handles and smooth-faced tail light lenses, and the introduction of more new engines. There were three of these, all from the modular family of 90-degree vee, three-valve types. Two were V6s, replacing the straight-sixes in the SL280 and SL320, and the third was a V8 that replaced the older V8 in the SL500. The SL600 remained available, and this four-model range continued until R129 production ended in summer 2001, the final months being marked by a special Silver Arrow edition of the SL500.

Over the years, there were AMG derivatives, too. Before the formal link with Mercedes in 1993, the tuner offered an AMG 500SL 6.0 model, with an enlarged V8 engine, but for the 1995 model year this became a

From the 1996 model year, the cars were characterised by different alloy wheels and by redesigned air vents on the wings.

The SL 600 with V12 engine topped the later range.

For real sporting performance, the later range incorporated an SL55 AMG model. This one was built in 1999.

catalogued model (with a few refinements) as the SL60 AMG. A second model was introduced in 1996, this time with a V12 engine bored and stroked to 7.3 litres and badged as an SL73 AMG. The SL60 AMG was replaced at the end of the 1997 season by an SL55 AMG, which of course used an engine available in other Mercedes-AMG models at the time.

Nearly 205,000 R129 models were built,

and figures show that annual average sales were around 4000 higher than those for the R107s. Far and away the best sellers of the range were the 5-litre V8 cars.

MODELS: SL280 (M104), SL280 (M112), 300SL, 300SL-24, SL320 (M104), SL320 (M112), 500SL, SL500 (M119), SL500 (M113), SL55 AMG, AMG 500SL 6.0, SL60 AMG, 600SL, SL600, SL73 AMG.

ENGINES: 2799cc M104 DOHC petrol six with 193PS (SL280); 2799cc M112 petrol V6 with 204PS (SL280); 2960cc M103 petrol six with 190PS (300SL); 2960cc M104 DOHC petrol six with 231PS (300SL-24); 3199cc M104 DOHC petrol six with 231PS (SL320); 3199cc M112 petrol V6 with 224PS (SL320); 4966cc M113 four-cam petrol V8 with 306PS (SL500); 4973cc M119 petrol V8 with 326PS, or (from 1995) 300PS (500SL & SL500); 5439cc M113 four-cam petrol V8 with 354PS (SL55 AMG); 5956cc M119 petrol V8 with 374PS, or (from 1996) 381PS (AMG 500SL 6.0 & SL60 AMG); 5987cc M120 petrol V12 with 394PS (600SL & SL600); 7291cc M120 petrol V12 with 525PS (SL73 AMG).

GEARBOX: Five-speed manual (SL280 only). Five-speed automatic

SUSPENSION, STEERING & BRAKES: Front suspension with MacPherson struts, wishbones, coil springs, and anti-roll bar. Rear suspension with five links, coil springs, and anti-roll bar. Self-levelling on all four wheels optional; adaptable dampers optional from 1990 and standard on SL600. Recirculating-ball steering with power assistance. Disc brakes all round with power assistance and ABS.

DIMENSIONS: Length: 4470mm (1990-1995 models); 4499mm (1996-2001 models). **Width:** 1812mm. **Height:** 1303mm with soft top, 1293mm with hardtop (to 1998); 1300mm with soft top, 1288mm with hardtop (from 1998); 1302mm with Panorama hardtop; 1296mm with soft top, 1286mm with hardtop (600SL/SL600); 1292mm with soft top, 1282mm with hardtop (SL60 AMG). **Wheelbase:** 2515mm. **Track:** 1535mm (front), 1523mm (rear), except: 1532mm (front), 1521mm (rear) for SL600, 1996-1998; 1567mm (front), 1557mm (rear) for SL60 AMG; 1553mm (front), 1545mm (rear) for SL55 AMG; 1553mm (front), 1541mm (rear) for SL73 AMG.

PERFORMANCE & FUEL CONSUMPTION: SL280 (both types): 140mph, 25mpg, 0-100km/h in 9.9 sec; 300SL: 138mph, 26mpg, 0-100km/h in 9.5 sec; 300SL-24: 143mph, 24mpg, 0-100km/h in 8.4 sec; SL320: (M104): 149mph, 24mpg, 0-100km/h in 8.4 sec; SL320 (M112): 148mph, 25mpg, 0-100km/h in 8.4 sec; 500SL (M119): 155mph (limited), 21mpg, 0-100km/h in 6.2 sec; SL500 (both types): 155mph (limited), 22mpg, 0-100km/h in 6.5 sec; SL55 AMG: 155mph (limited), 21mpg, 0-100km/h in 5.9 sec; SL600: 155mph (limited), 12mpg, 0-100km/h in 6.1 sec; SL73 AMG: 191mph(*), 12mpg, 0-100km/h in 4.8 sec.
(*) early cars limited to 155mph.

PRODUCTION TOTALS: SL280 (M104): 10,319; SL280 (M112): 1704; 300SL: 12,020; 300SL-24: 26,984; SL320 (M104): 32,223; SL320 (M112): 7070; 500SL & SL500 (M119): 79,827; SL500 (M113): 23,704; 600SL/SL600: 11,089.
Figures for AMG models are included with their 'host' type; eg the 85 SL73 AMG cars are included in the total for the SL600.

The R170 SLK, 1996-2004

By the end of the 1980s, car makers everywhere were once again contemplating the possibilities of an affordable two-seater sports model. The threat of such cars being outlawed by safety legislation in the USA had kept them off the market for the best part of two decades, but had now receded. While most makers merely contemplated, Japanese maker Mazda acted, and the huge success of its 1989 MX-5 roadster made clear that the time was right for others to follow suit.

The 'junior SL' was a desirable sports car in its own right. This is a right-hand-drive car registered in the UK. (Nik Grewer)

There was an air of lightness, almost cheekiness, about the rear view of the SLK. This is an early SLK200 model.

Mercedes nevertheless hesitated, and did not decide to produce a small sports two-seater until 1992. The R170 programme was set up to produce this 'junior SL', which had to be very different from the traditional SL that was not only well established but also very much more expensive. The most cost-effective way of creating such a car was to base it on the platform of the W202 compact saloon that was then under development, and Mercedes decided that it would have to appeal to younger buyers. A youthful, almost cheeky body style was therefore drawn up, complemented by an innovative power-operated retractable steel hardtop that would replace the traditional SL combination of a folding soft top and a removable hardtop. In production, this would be called the Vario roof.

To prepare the market for what was coming, a pair of fully functional concept models were displayed at motor shows during 1994, one at the Turin in April and the second at Paris in October. Both had show-car features that were not intended to make production but would draw attention, while also giving a good idea of the essentials of the forthcoming car. They went down extremely well, and by the time the car actually went on sale two years later, Mercedes was able to claim advance orders for 25,000 examples.

The new R170 was released with a choice of three engines, all four-cylinders. The entry-level SLK200 had 136PS; the top model SLK230 Kompressor with its supercharged engine had 193PS; and for markets where a 2-litre capacity limit was dictated by tax regulations there was a 192PS

SLK200 Kompressor. Gearboxes were five-speed manuals as standard, and there was an automatic option. Space in the boot was compromised when the roof was retracted, and these were the first Mercedes ever to be sold without a proper spare wheel; some countries received a 'space saver' spare wheel but other merely had a can of tyre sealant and an electric pump.

There was no reason to make major changes in the R170's first four years, and revised models were not introduced until February 2000. There was a minor face-lift, which added turn signals in the door mirrors but mainly affected the front end and details of the passenger cabin, and there were two new engines. The SLK230 Kompressor remained the core model while the whole range moved up a step. The new entry-level model was a less powerful (163PS) version of the SLK200 Kompressor and a new six-cylinder model took

As was now the Mercedes tradition, the top performance model was developed by AMG. This SLK32 AMG also has its folding Vario Roof erected.

This SLK Final Edition shows how the car had matured over the years to develop its own identity, quite different from that of the larger SL.

the SLK into new territory. The six-cylinder was called the SLK320 and had a 218PS version of the V6 engine available in several other Mercedes models. At the same time, all the face-lifted cars took on a six-speed manual gearbox as standard.

The success of the SLK320 persuaded Mercedes to explore whether an even higher-performance model would find acceptance, and from 2001 the range was topped out by a new SLK32 AMG, which would always be built in limited quantities. Its engine was, once again, the 3.2-litre V6, but this time supercharged by Mercedes' AMG performance division to give a huge 354PS. This car claimed the title of the fastest-accelerating volume-production Mercedes ever built. It was distinguished by special wheels, an enlarged front air intake, a lip spoiler on the boot lid, and some special interior features.

These four models carried the R170 range through to the end of production in 2004. The best seller had been the 143mph SLK200 Kompressor, and the overall success of the range both proved the rightness of the Mercedes approach and informed the shape of the R171 SLK range that succeeded the R170s.

MODELS: SLK200: (1996-2000); SLK200 Kompressor: (1996-2004); SLK230

Kompressor: (1996-2004); SLK320: (2000-2004); SLK 32 AMG: (2000-2004).

ENGINES: 1998cc M111 petrol four with 136PS (SLK200); 1998cc M111 supercharged petrol four with 192PS, or (from 2000) 163PS (SLK200 Kompressor); 2295cc M111 petrol four with 193PS, or (from 2000) 197PS (SLK230 Kompressor); 3199cc M112 petrol V6 with 218PS (SLK320); 3199cc M112 supercharged petrol V6 with 354 PS (SLK32 AMG).

GEARBOXES: Five-speed manual (to 1999). Six-speed manual (from 2000). Five-speed automatic.

SUSPENSION, STEERING & BRAKES: Front suspension with twin unequal-length wishbones, coil springs, and anti-roll bar. Rear suspension with five links and coil springs. Rack-and-pinion steering with power assistance. Disc brakes all round, ventilated at the front on all models, and on SLK320 and SLK32 AMG at the rear as well; power assistance and ABS.

DIMENSIONS: Length: 3995mm or (from 2000) 4010mm. **Width:** 1715mm. **Height:** 1269-1284mm. **Wheelbase:** 2400mm. **Track:** 1488mm (front), 1471-1485mm (rear).

PERFORMANCE & FUEL CONSUMPTION: Figures for manual gearbox models unless otherwise indicated.

*The Vario Roof is erect in this picture of the Final Edition.
It was always power-operated.*

SLK200: 129mph, 31mpg, 0-100km/h in 9.3 sec; SLK200 Kompressor: 143mph, 31mpg, 0-100km/h in 7.7 sec; SLK230 Kompressor: 149mph, 30mpg, 0-100km/h in 7.2 sec; SLK230 Kompressor auto: 141mph, 29.5mpg, 0-100km/h in 7.3 sec; SLK320: 152mph, 25.5mpg, 0-100km/h in 6.9 sec; SLK320 auto: 150mph, 27mpg, 0-100km/h in 6.9 sec; SLK32 AMG: 155mph (limited), 25mpg, 0-100km/h in 5.2 sec.
PRODUCTION TOTALS: SLK200: 44,846; SLK 200 Kompressor: 125,873; SLK 230 Kompressor: 102,754; SLK 320: 33,416; SLK 32 AMG: 4333.

*The almost pert appearance was maintained to the end. As the badge makes clear, this Final
Edition was an SLK230.*

The 170S cabriolet, 1949-1951

It was not until 1949 that Mercedes believed it could risk producing a cabriolet model – a car that a few years previously would have been considered frivolous and against the national requirement for basic transport.

The idea that this was a somewhat self-indulgent luxury that only the wealthy might be able to afford nevertheless dominated, and the cabriolet models were developed as the Mercedes flagships of their time. This is why they were based on the new 170S chassis rather than the entry-level 170V or 170D. They would retain that flagship status only briefly as the West German economy continued to recover, but for around two years, these were the most expensive Mercedes on offer.

There were actually two different models, which used the traditional German nomenclature of Cabriolet A (for the two-seater model which had luggage space behind the seats) and Cabriolet B (for the more spacious five-seater). Both were intended primarily for export, even though the increasing stability of the West German economy had been behind their conception, and in the event the Cabriolet B model outsold the Cabriolet A by around two to one. Even so, overall sales were not large, with an annual average of just over 1000 cars.

Like the 170S saloon that was their contemporary, these cars were designated W136 models by the factory. They went out of production in 1951, giving way to new six-cylinder 220S cabriolets.

With the open models of the 170S, Mercedes gingerly re-entered the market for cars that were more than pure modes of transport. This is a Cabriolet A.

Advertising material for 170S Cabriolet A carefully played to potential customers. The car looked most attractive from this angle.

MODELS: 170S Cabriolet A, 170S Cabriolet B.
ENGINE: 1767cc petrol four with 52PS.
GEARBOX: Four-speed all-synchromesh manual.
SUSPENSION, STEERING & BRAKES: Twin wishbones at the front, with coil springs and anti-roll bar; swing axles at the rear with coil springs. Worm steering. Drum brakes on all four wheels.

When four or five seats were needed, the Cabriolet B provided the answer. The external landau irons were typical of German cabriolets at the time.

The 170S Cabriolet B had a determinedly substantial look, especially when finished in sober black like this one.

DIMENSIONS: Length: 4510mm (Cabriolet A); 4455mm (Cabriolet B). **Width:** 1684mm. **Height:** 1610mm. **Wheelbase:** 2845mm. **Track:** 1315mm (front); 1420mm (rear).
PERFORMANCE & FUEL CONSUMPTION: All models: 76mph, 19mpg, 0-100km/h in 32 sec.
PRODUCTION TOTALS: Cabriolet A: 830; Cabriolet B: 1603.

The 220 cabriolet and coupé, 1951-1955

Once the W187 220S six-cylinder model entered development, it was probably a foregone conclusion that the core saloon model should be accompanied by cabriolet derivatives and that these should replace the 170S types that were then the top models of the Mercedes range.

So it was that two cabriolet models were announced with the 220S saloon in 1951. These were a two/three-seater Cabriolet A and a five-seater Cabriolet B. The pretty Cabriolet A was more expensive than the more practical Cabriolet B and sold better – which gives an idea of the appeal of these cars at the time.

From 1954, the two cabriolets were joined by a fixed-head coupé that was based on the two/three-seater body of the Cabriolet A. This became the most expensive model in the 220S range, and could be ordered with a sliding steel sunroof at extra cost. Its late arrival and elevated price ensured that it would be by far the slowest seller, which of course enhances its rarity today.

The Cabriolet A on the six-cylinder 220S was very similar to its counterpart on the four-cylinder chassis.

This superb example of a 220S survives in a German museum. The '220 B' on the number-plate indicates that it is a Cabriolet B variant of the 220.

Once again determinedly substantial, this is the five-seater cabriolet on the six-cylinder chassis.

The 220 coupé was a late arrival, and essentially added a fixed roof to the Cabriolet A body.

Production ended in 1955, leaving a one-year hiatus before the next generation of Mercedes' exclusive middle-class cabriolets and coupés would appear as derivatives of the Ponton range.

MODELS: 220 Cabriolet A, 220 Cabriolet B,: 220 coupé.
ENGINE: 2195cc M180 petrol six with 80PS.
GEARBOX: Four-speed all-synchromesh manual.
SUSPENSION, STEERING & BRAKES: Twin wishbones at the front, with coil springs and anti-roll bar; swing axles at the rear with double coil springs. Worm steering. Drum brakes on all four wheels.
DIMENSIONS: Length: 4538mm (Cabriolet A). **Width:** 1685mm. **Height:** 1560mm (Cabriolet A). **Wheelbase:** 2845mm. **Track:** 1315mm (front), 1485mm (rear).
PERFORMANCE & FUEL CONSUMPTION: Saloon: 90mph, 16mpg, 0-100km/h in 21.0 sec.
PRODUCTION TOTALS: 1278 Cabriolet A; 997 Cabriolet B; 85 coupé.

The 300S cabriolets, coupés & roadsters, 1951-1958

The 300S was developed alongside the big 300 limousine as an exclusive personal car for the very wealthy and was announced shortly after it at the 1951 Paris Show, although volume production did not begin until July 1952. Based on a shorter-wheelbase version of the 300's chassis, the 300S had its own unique factory designation of W188.

It also had a more powerful three-carburettor version of the 3-litre engine with 150PS, different gearing, and finned brake drums (which were supplemented by a servo from mid-1953). With a 110mph top speed it was bested only by the 300SL Gullwing coupé, but it cost more and always sold in smaller numbers.

There were three versions of the 300S, which came as a roadster, a Cabriolet A or a fixed-head coupé. All cost the same – almost 1.75 times as much as a 300 limousine – and for nearly six years the 300S was West Germany's most expensive production car. Sales slowed down in 1954 after the Gullwing model arrived, but received a boost in 1956 when the sports car's injected engine was installed to create what was known internally as the 300Sc. (The model preceded the injected 300d limousine by a year.) With 175PS, the new engine added only 2mph to the top speed but delivered much greater flexibility than its triple-carburettor predecessor.

This was the 300S cabriolet, here looking every bit as superbly finished as it was in the metal.

The roadster version of the 300S could be recognised by the absence of a folded hood behind the seats.

When the injected engine reached the prestige two-door models, they were internally renamed 300Sc types. This is the coupé.

What better way of advertising the extra power behind by carrying a badge reading 'Einspritzmotor' (injected engine)? This is again a 300Sc coupé. (Rex Gray, CCA 2.0)

The buyer enthusiasm of 1956 was short-lived, however. Sales soon dropped alarmingly and Mercedes decided to withdraw the model altogether in 1958, allowing the recently introduced 300SL roadster to take up much of the slack. Interestingly, however, the roadster variants of the 300S were always the slowest sellers, and it was the coupé that sold most strongly.

MODELS: Roadster, Coupé, Cabriolet A and Cabriolet B, 300S, 300Sc.
ENGINES: 2996cc M186 petrol six with 150PS (300S). 2996cc M189 petrol six with 175PS and fuel-injection (300Sc).
GEARBOX: Four-speed all-synchromesh manual
SUSPENSION, STEERING & BRAKES: Twin wishbones at the front, with coil springs and anti-roll bar; swing axles at the rear with coil springs; single-pivot type on 300Sc. Recirculating-ball steering. Drum brakes on all four wheels, with servo assistance from 1954.
DIMENSIONS: Length: 4700mm. **Width:** 1860mm. **Height:** 1510mm. **Wheelbase:** 2900mm. **Track:** 1480mm (front); 1525mm (rear).

PERFORMANCE & FUEL CONSUMPTION: 300S: 109mph, 14mpg, 0-100km/h in 15.0 sec; 300Sc: 112mph, 14mpg, 0-100km/h in 14.0 sec.
PRODUCTION TOTALS: 300S coupé: 216 300S Cabriolet A: 203; 300S roadster: 141; 300Sc coupé: 98; 300Sc Cabriolet A: 49; 300Sc roadster: 53.

The Ponton cabriolets and coupés, 1956-1960

Cabriolet and coupé derivatives of the Ponton range were only to be expected after the last separate-chassis 220S two-door models were withdrawn in 1955. The first 'teaser' for the new models was a cabriolet badged as a 220 and shown at the Frankfurt Show in autumn 1955, but the plan was probably always to use the more powerful 220S engine – which at that stage had not been announced. Demand was allowed to build up over the next few months, and the cabriolet 220S previewed both the new engine and the new two-door cars in July 1956.

The prestige two-door models had little in common visually with the Ponton saloons from which they were derived. This 220S has a two-tone option.

Peaks over the tail lamps added a special touch of style at the rear of the two-doors, which positively oozed luxury from this angle.

Heavily padded seats upholstered in leather, and a swathe of wood for the dashboard confirmed to passengers that these were luxury models.

They also shared the saloon's W180 factory designation, but were very different cars that sat on a shorter wheelbase and had styling that was only distantly related to that of the saloons and featured a wraparound

The coupé models shared their lower body with the cabriolets, adding a neatly styled roof with wrapover rear window.
(Emslichter, Pixabay)

windscreen. Two cabriolet models were made available, but in reality they were the same except for their seats: the Cabriolet A had a luggage shelf behind its front seats while the Cabriolet C had a properly upholstered bench seat instead. This saved the cost of engineering major differences, which with monocoque construction would have been considerable. The coupé that joined the range in September 1956 bore witness to the same cost-conscious approach, and was really a cabriolet with a fixed roof.

These were still very expensive cars, hand-finished at Sindelfingen in the tradition of Mercedes' top models. They were available with a wider variety of colour options than the contemporary saloons, and these included

Two-colour paintwork and plenty of brightwork made these cars stand out when they were new. This is a rare injected 220SE model. (Stahlkocher, GNU Free Documentation Licence)

some stylish two-tone paint schemes that reflected the contemporary American fashion for such things. Many customers, of course, were in America.

In original form, these two-door models lasted until 1959, when the carburettor 220S versions were withdrawn in favour of injected 220SE models that had been announced in 1958. These new types were essentially the same as their predecessors, but they shared their W128 factory designation with their 220SE saloon contemporaries. They remained on sale until 1960, by which time their even more magnificent replacements were waiting in the wings.

MODELS: Coupé, Cabriolet A and Cabriolet C 220S.
ENGINES: 2195cc M180 petrol six with 100PS or 106PS from August 1957; 2195cc M127 petrol six with injection and 115PS.
GEARBOXES: Four-speed manual, all-synchromesh. Hydrak automatic clutch optional from August 1957.
SUSPENSION, STEERING & BRAKES: Front suspension with twin wishbones and coil springs. Rear suspension with single-pivot swing-axles and coil springs. Recirculating-ball steering, unassisted. Drum brakes on all four wheels, with vacuum servo as standard.
DIMENSIONS: Length: 4670mm. **Width:** 1765mm. **Height:** 1530mm. **Wheelbase:** 2700mm. **Track:** 1430mm (front), 1470mm (rear).
PERFORMANCE & FUEL CONSUMPTION: 220S: 99mph, 21mpg, 0-100km/h in 17.0 sec; 220SE: 99mph, 22mpg, 0-100km/h in 15.0 sec.
PRODUCTION TOTALS: 220S Cabriolet (A&C): 2178; 220S coupé: 1251; 220SE Cabriolet (A&C): 1112; 220SE coupé: 830.

The Fintail cabriolets and coupés, 1961-1971

Among the most admired classic Mercedes are the big four-seater cabriolets and coupés that were based on the Fintail saloons. They are sometimes also called Fintail models themselves, but Paul Bracq's elegant styling had very little in common with that of the parent saloons. This ancestry nevertheless ensured that they would retain the W111 (and later W112) designation way beyond the end of Fintail saloon production.

Unlike the two-door range based on the Ponton models, this one retained the standard wheelbase to give the cars a spacious and luxurious seating compartment. Coupés and cabriolets shared the same basic shape, with full-drop side windows that allowed the coupés to be seen as hardtops in the USA. Bracq's design was lower, more rounded, and sleeker than that of its saloon contemporaries, and from the start had an indefinable timeless quality about it.

The first cars were coupés, released in 1961 at the same Geneva Show as Jaguar's E-type; cabriolets followed that autumn. All were 220SE types with the injected 2.2-litre six-cylinder engine and a choice of manual or automatic gearbox. Front disc brakes were standard from the start and the 220SE coupé was therefore the first Mercedes to have them. Then from March 1962, new flagship versions of the two-door models became available with the 300SE (W112) specification that included air suspension and the injected alloy 3-litre engine.

From 1965, the mechanical specification of new two-door variants was aligned with that of the W108 and W109 models. The 220SE gave way to a 250SE that year, and

These two-door models shared nothing obvious with the parent saloons. This early 220SE coupé has the optional two-tone paintwork.

This time in a single colour, a 220SE shows the lines that have made these cars coveted classics today.

The cabriolets shared the same timeless lines as the coupés, again offering luxury accommodation for four. This is another early 220SE.

The 300SE models that topped the early range were distinguished by additional brightwork.

then in turn to a 280SE in 1967. Production of the 300SE also ended in 1967, and it would be two years before a new top model was introduced, this time with the brand-new 3.5-litre V8 engine and badged as a 280SE 3.5. In emissions-controlled form for North America, the V8 model was not markedly quicker than the six-cylinder, but Mercedes distinguished it with a lower and wider radiator grille and rubber bumper inserts.

Although North American saloon models would regain lost performance with an enlarged 4.5-litre V8 engine in spring 1971, the coupés and cabriolets did not. They stayed with the 3.5-litre engine until their production ended later that year – by which time they had become magnificent anachronisms.

MODELS: Coupé and cabriolet: 220SE, 250SE, 280SE, 280SE 3.5, 300SE.

ENGINES: 2195cc M127 petrol six with injection and 120PS (220SE); 2496cc M129 petrol six with injection and 150PS (250SE); 2778cc M130 petrol six with injection and 160PS (280SE); 2996cc M189 petrol six with injection and 170PS (300SE); 3499cc M116 petrol V8 with injection and 200PS (280SE 3.5).

GEARBOXES: Four-speed manual, all-synchromesh. Four-speed automatic option.

SUSPENSION, STEERING & BRAKES: Front suspension with twin wishbones, coil springs and anti-roll bar. Rear suspension with single-pivot swing axle and coil springs. Recirculating-ball steering, unassisted; optional power assistance (standard on 300SE). Disc brakes on all four wheels, except 220S & 220SE with drums on the rear wheels.

DIMENSIONS: Length: 4880mm or 4905mm (280SE 3.5). **Width:** 1845mm. **Height:** 1445mm (220SE); 1420mm 250SE & 280SE coupé, 1435mm. 250SE &280SE cabriolet; 1405mm (280SE 3.5 coupé); 1420mm (280SE 3.5 cabriolet); 1400mm (300SE). **Wheelbase:** 2750mm. **Track:** 1482mm (front); 1485mm (rear).

PERFORMANCE & FUEL CONSUMPTION: 220SE: 107mph, 16mpg (15mpg automatic), 0-100km/h in 14 sec; 250SE manual 120mph, 15mpg, 0-100km/h in 12 sec; 250SE automatic: 117mph, 14mpg, 0-100km/h in 12 sec; 280SE manual:

By the time of this 1970 US-specification coupé, the two-door models had the 280SE designation. (Mr.choppers, CC-by-SA 3.0)

Apparently another US-specification car, despite the German plates, this cabriolet is a late-model 280SE 3.5 with the V8 engine. (Alexander Migl, CC-by-SA 4.0)

Hugely respected and coveted today, this is a 1971 US-model 280SE 3.5 cabriolet, seen with the top erect. (Classicsworkshop, CC-by-SA 4.0)

120mph, 15mpg, 0-100km/h in 11 sec; 280SE automatic: 117mph, 14mpg, 0-100km/h in 11 sec; 280SE3.5: 130mph, 13mpg, 0-100km/h in 10 sec; 300SE (160PS): 112mph (109mph automatic), 12-14mpg, 0-100km/h in 13 sec; 300SE (170PS): 118mph (115mph automatic), 12-14mpg, 0-100km/h in 12 sec.

PRODUCTION TOTALS: 220SE cabriolet & coupé: 16,902; 250SE cabriolet & coupé: 6213; 280SE cabriolet & coupé: 5187; 280SE 3.5 cabriolet & coupé: 4502: 300SE cabriolet & coupé: 3127.

The Stroke 8 coupés, 1969-1976

Severawl European car makers started work on coupé versions of their medium-range saloons in the mid-1960s in order to capitalise on the American vogue for pillarless hardtops. The Mercedes take on this fashion was to develop a junior companion to the big luxury coupés and cabriolets based on the Fintail range that were scheduled to remain in production for several more years. The fashion did not call for a cabriolet model at this level of the market, but Mercedes decided that its new junior coupés would have the prestige of six-cylinder engines. That would also help to distinguish them from the four-cylinder models that Ford and Opel were developing for Europe.

The new coupés could obviously be based on the new saloons then in preparation, which were the 'Stroke 8' models scheduled for 1968 introduction. To maximise commonality of both visual and mechanical elements,

The W114 coupés were another well-resolved design, in this case deliberately resembling their parent saloons.

Characteristic of these cars was a long rear deck, which is seen here on a 1970 250CE Automatic in Australia. (jeremy, CC-by-SA 2.0)

American regulations had an impact on these cars, and this US-model 280C has the special lighting arrangements required across the Atlantic. (IFCAR, Public Domain)

Paul Bracq's studio did not begin work on these cars until the saloons had been signed off. The plan was that they should have the same wheelbase as the saloons, and retain essentially the same shape below the waistline (although they would have two rather than four doors). The new visual element was therefore the sleek hardtop roof, with bright metal bars that gave a family resemblance to the hardtop for the W113 Pagoda sports models.

It must be said that this arrangement made for a rather long rear deck – ideal for luggage, perhaps, but not a complete visual success. The coupés were given double bumpers to help distinguish them more readily from the new saloons, but they retained very much the same interior, with seats adapted to suit the reduced headroom and the front pair tipping to allow rear-seat access.

The first Stroke 8 coupés were made public at the Geneva Show in March 1969 – although some members of the press had been given a preview six months earlier. They came as two models, both W114 types, which were badged as 250C and 250CE. The 250C had the same 130PS engine as the top-model Stroke 8 saloon, but to give the coupé range a cachet of its own the 250CE came with the latest Bosch fuel-injection and an extra 20PS. A little more exclusivity came from the availability of metallic paints, some five years before these filtered down to the Stroke 8 saloons, and of course the big options list also included a series of two-tone paint finishes. Although the standard gearbox was a four-speed manual, these were deliberately prestigious cars, and most customers ordered the alternative four-speed automatic, which at this stage was driven through a fluid flywheel.

These coupés arrived at a time when new US regulations about crash safety, lighting, and emissions were all coming into force. Annual changes to those regulations required annual changes to the cars, and although some changes could be incorporated on models for all territories, others were restricted to cars destined for the USA. As a result, the Stroke 8 coupé model range became more than a little complicated over the next few years.

At the start of the 1970 season in mid-1969, the main news on a global basis was the availability of a five-speed overdrive gearbox (although the automatic remained the popular choice) and of Fuchs 'Mexican hat' alloy wheels. It was at this point that the cars were introduced to the USA, however, and while other markets still had the 250C and 250CE, US buyers were offered just one model, their own very different version of the 250C. Special lighting arrangements aside, these cars had the new 2.8-litre carburettor engine with 130PS – the same output as the European model with a 300cc smaller engine.

The next major model change came in April 1972, and there was now a choice of three core models, which were called 250C, 280C and 280CE. The 250C for all markets now took on the 130PS carburettor 2.8-litre engine. The other two models had the new M110 twin-cam 2.8-litre engine, the 280C with carburettors and 160PS and the 280CE with injection and 185PS. Once again, the USA went its own way with a single model, which had a 120PS twin-cam 2.8-litre engine with single carburettor and was badged as a 280C.

Just over a year after that came the face-lift for the whole W114 (and W115) range. All the coupés took on the new wider grille, ribbed

Later US models required extended bumpers as well. Here they are on a 1976 280C. (Greg Gjerdingen/WikiMedia Commons)

rear light lenses, and larger door mirrors with fixed quarter-lights, while a torque-converter four-speed automatic gearbox replaced the earlier fluid-flywheel type. Although the range of models remained the same, the face-lift was accompanied for the 1974-season US 280C by huge bumpers mounted on compression struts, which did nothing for the visual balance of the design.

The oil crisis that followed immediately afterwards led to a worldwide drop in sales of these coupés. Then tighter emissions regulations in the US state of California for the 1975 season were met by the addition of catalytic converters and by engines that revved higher to achieve peak power – leading to a reduction of refinement. Production of the final models – the 280C in 49-State and Californian forms, and the 280C and 280CE for the rest of the world – was finally brought to an end in summer 1976.

MODELS: 250C, 250C (2.8), 250CE, 280C, 280CE.
ENGINES: 2496cc M114 petrol six with 130PS (250C, to 1976); 2496cc M114 petrol six with 150PS and fuel-injection (250CE); 2746cc M110 DOHC six with 120PS (280C for USA); 2746cc M110 DOHC six with 160PS (280C); 2746cc M110 DOHC six with 185PS and fuel-injection (280CE); 2778cc M130 petrol six with 130PS (250C, 1969-1973).
GEARBOXES: Four-speed manual standard. Five-speed manual optional. Four-speed automatic.
SUSPENSION, STEERING & BRAKES:
Front suspension with twin wishbones, coil springs and anti-roll bar. Rear suspension with

'diagonal swing axle' (semi-trailing arms), coil springs, rubber auxiliary springs and anti-roll bar. Optional hydro-pneumatic self-levelling strut. Recirculating ball steering; optional power assistance. Disc brakes on all four wheels.

DIMENSIONS: Length: 4680mm. **Width:** 1790mm. **Height:** 1395mm. **Wheelbase:** 2750mm . **Track:** 1448mm (front), 1440mm (rear).

PERFORMANCE & FUEL CONSUMPTION: 250C manual: 115mph, 18mpg, 0-100km/h in 13 sec; 250C automatic: 112mph, 17mpg, 0-100km/h in 13 sec; 250CE manual: 121mph, 18mpg, 0-100km/h in 11 sec; 250CE automatic: 118mph, 17mpg, 0-100km/h in 11 sec; 250C (2.8) manual: 112mph, 18mpg, 0-100km/h in 13 sec; 250C (2.8) auto: 109mph, 17mpg, 0-100km/h in 13 sec; 280C manual: 118mph, 18mpg, 0-100km/h in 11 sec; 280C automatic: 118mph, 17mpg, 0-100km/h in 11 sec; 280CE manual: 124mph, 18mpg, 0-100km/h in 10 sec; 280CE automatic: 124mph, 17mpg, 0-100km/h in 10 sec.

PRODUCTION TOTALS: 250C: 8824; 250C (2.8): 11,768; 250CE: 21,787; 280C: 13,151; 280CE: 11,518.

The C107 SLC, 1972-1981

When Mercedes started work on replacements for the big Fintail-based coupés and cabriolets, new American regulations concerning exhaust emissions and safety were about to kick in. Meeting them was certainly going to incur additional development costs, and Mercedes estimated that adding a coupé derivative to the logical parent range (the new W116 S Class) would delay the whole programme by a year.

There was, nevertheless, scope within the programme for the 107-series SL Roadsters, and so the bold decision was taken to base the flagship coupé model on that instead. The idea was to create a long-wheelbase, four-seater version of the basic 107 design,

The SLC was really an extended-wheelbase SL with a hardtop, but it was also a beautiful and sleek design.

This US-specification car has the twin round headlamps and extended bumpers required by local regulations, along with alloy wheels.

Another US car, a 450SLC, shows the treatment of the rearmost side windows and the tail end of these models. (Mr.choppers, CC-by-SA 3.0)

but there would be no cabriolet equivalent. The main reason was that the extra body strengthening needed would raise weight unacceptably.

The new coupé was designated C107 to distinguish it from the R107 roadster, and room for the extra seats was created by adding 360mm (14.2in) to the wheelbase. The front end panelling, the rear details, and even the doors were essentially taken directly from the roadster, as was the dashboard and control layout. The coupé's special features were its longer roof, wraparound rear window and interesting side window treatment with louvres behind the side glass; these were chosen because they looked better than the quarter-light that would have otherwise been necessary to allow the window to drop fully and maintain the desired 'hardtop' configuration. The bench rear seat was just about large enough for two, but the car was really a 2+2 rather than a full four-seater.

The C107 was announced about six months after the R107 roadsters (see p65, at the October 1971 Paris Motor Show. Sales began in January 1972 and the last cars were built in 1981. The replacements for the coupés were based on the latest S Class saloons although the R107s remained in production for another eight years. As a result, there were only two generations of C107 as against three of the R107.

Like the roadsters, the coupés entered production in V8-engined 350SLC form, but US models were delayed until summer 1972, and had the 4.5-litre engine to counter power losses caused by emissions control equipment – though still with 350SLC

badges. All the US models had a three-speed torque-converter automatic gearbox, but elsewhere the choice with the 3.5-litre engine was between a four-speed manual and the more popular four-speed fluid-flywheel automatic. All that was rationalised later, when a full-fat 450SLC became available outside the USA alongside the 350SLC; the US model was renamed a 450SLC, and all models took on the three-speed gearbox as the automatic option.

Again, exactly like the roadsters, a six-cylinder 280SLC had been planned for export to those countries where the size of the V8 engines would make them unsaleable. This model was released in 1974 as the effects of the oil crisis were being felt, and helped keep sales alive in a rather different way from that originally intended. There were, however, none for either the USA or the UK.

While the 280SLC, 350SLC and 450SLC continued in production, Mercedes chose to use its flagship coupé to showcase a number of ideas intended for future models. A new limited-production variant was developed that was shown at the Frankfurt Show in autumn 1977 as the 450SLC 5.0. As the name suggested, it had a new 5.0-litre V8 engine, closely related to the cast iron 4.5-litre M117, but in this case made of light alloy to save weight. Its combustion system was optimised for fuel economy, and servicing requirements were reduced by the use of hydraulic tappets. Lightweight alloy body panels trimmed further weight and a tall axle ratio gave this new SLC a 140mph top speed as well as better acceleration and better fuel economy than the regular 450SLC.

The 280SLC remained available until the end of C107 production in 1981, but the 450SLC 5.0 lasted only until the end of first-generation SLC production in 1980. In the autumn of that year, the 350SLC and 450SLC joined the roadsters in switching to the new lightweight alloy V8 engines, becoming 380SLC and 500SLC models respectively. The 500SLC's engine was slightly revised as compared to that of the 450SLC 5.0, and (again as with the SL roadsters) the 3.8-litre engine had different bore and stroke dimensions for the USA to minimise noxious exhaust emissions. Both these new models also had the light-alloy panels of the 450SLC 5.0, and could be ordered with an ABS braking system. Only early examples of the 380SLC had the original European-specification engine, and the last ones (from spring 1981) had the Europeanised long-stroke 3.8-litre V8 first used in the US models.

The expedient of basing the flagship coupé on the SL roadster never did meet the approval of every member of Mercedes top management, and the plan to base its replacement on the top-model saloons was formulated quite early on. Nevertheless, the SLC models were worthy if slightly inconspicuous flagships of their time, often taking on specification improvements before the equivalent roadster models and typically being sold with rather higher levels of equipment and extras.

MODELS: 280SLC, 350SLC, 380SLC, 450SLC, 450SLC 5.0, 500SLC.

ENGINES: 2746cc M110 DOHC petrol six with 185PS (280SLC); 3499cc M116 petrol V8 with 200PS (350SLC); 3818cc M116 petrol V8 with 218PS (380SLC); 4520cc M117 petrol V8 with 225PS (450SLC); 4973cc M117 petrol V8 with 245PS (500SLC); 5025cc M117 petrol V8 with 240PS (450SLC 5.0).
GEARBOXES: Four-speed manual. Five-speed manual (280SLC option). Three-speed automatic (450SLC). Four-speed automatic.
SUSPENSION, STEERING & BRAKES: Front suspension with wishbones, coil springs and anti-roll bar. Rear suspension with semi-trailing arms, coil springs and anti-roll bar; hydraulic self-levelling optional from July 1972. Recirculating-ball steering with power assistance. Disc brakes all round with power assistance.
DIMENSIONS: Length: 4750mm. **Width:** 1790mm. **Height:** 1330mm. **Wheelbase:** 2820mm. **Track:** 1452mm (front), 1440mm (rear).
PERFORMANCE & FUEL CONSUMPTION: 280SLC manual: 127mph, 18mpg, 0-100km/h in 10 sec; 280SLC auto: 127mph, 18mpg, 0-100km/h in 11 sec; 350SLC manual: 132mph, 15mpg, 0-100km/h in 9 sec; 350SLC auto: 132mph, 15mpg, 0-100km/h in 10 sec; 380SLC: 133mph, 15mpg, 0-100km/h in 9.5 sec; 450SLC: 135mph, 15mpg, 0-100km/h in 9.5 sec; 450SLC 5.0 & 500SLC: 140mph, 15mpg, 0-100km/h in 8.5 sec.
PRODUCTION TOTALS: 280SLC 10,666; 350SLC: 13,925; 380SLC: 3789; 450SLC: 31,739; 450SLC 5.0 & 500SLC: 2769.

The 450SLC 5.0 was distinguished by its discreet tail spoiler and by blacked-out lower panels.

Like their W114 predecessors, the C123 models had a close visual relationship to the saloons on which they were based.

The C123 coupés, 1977-1985

The successors to the W114 coupés took on the C123 designation, once again as hardtop models that were closely related to the parent saloons. Yet there were important differences: this time they were based on a shortened platform to improve aesthetics, and instead of an all-six-cylinder range they were planned to have both four- and six-cylinder engines. Also planned – and a surprise when it appeared – was a five-cylinder diesel variant that was built only for the USA.

The wheelbase was shorter than that of the saloons. This is a six-cylinder 280CE.

This UK-registered C123 is a four-cylinder 230CE, although it was impossible to distinguish between the two coupé models from this angle.

Extended bumpers did nothing for the looks of the US-model coupés. This one is a petrol 280CE. (Mr.choppers, CC-by-SA 3.0)

Styling work began during 1972, by which time the lines of the parent saloons had been fairly clearly established, and was complete by September 1973. Four-cylinder and six-cylinder coupés alike were to have the cosmetic appearance of the top-model saloons, with rectangular headlamps and wraparound bumpers, and they would also have the low-profile tyres that were otherwise found only on the most expensive W123 saloons. The interior was very much based on the saloon type, but with plenty of wood trim to support the models' luxury status, plus tipping front seats to give rear access and a rear seat shaped for just two passengers.

The new coupés were announced in January 1977, a year after the saloons, and went on public display at the Geneva show that March. Three models entered production, a four-cylinder 230C, an injected six-cylinder 280CE, and there was a carburettor 280C for some countries. All came with a choice of manual or automatic gearboxes. Sales actually began in June 1977 but there were no coupés for the USA until 1978, when two models, both with automatic gearboxes, went on sale.

The US model range was complicated by the need for different 49-state and California specifications, to meet differing emission requirements. So the 280CE came with either 142bhp or 137bhp (as against 185PS in European tune). The second US model

fitted into the Mercedes plan to reduce the overall fuel consumption of its US models by using diesel engines, and was a 300CD with the five-cylinder diesel engine and a miserable 77bhp (80PS). It was uprated to 89bhp (88PS) a year later to aid sales, but despite the mismatch between coupé image and diesel performance, the climate of the times allowed it to become accepted as an environmentally responsible luxury model.

There were only minor specification changes for the C123s over the next couple of years, and, although there were engine changes for the saloons in autumn 1979, the coupés had to wait another year before a 230CE with the new M102 engine replaced the carburettor 230C. The 280C was then withdrawn in summer 1980, leaving three models in production – 230CE, 280CE, and 300CD for the USA.

The US success of the turbocharged five-cylinder diesel engine in the 300TD Turbodiesel persuaded Mercedes to put this into the US coupés from summer 1981, and for 1982 the 300CD was replaced by a 300CD Turbodiesel. As before, there were 49-state and Californian models, with 125bhp and 118bhp respectively. The 280CE disappeared from the US line-up for 1982, but remained available elsewhere alongside the 230CE.

A further change, this time affecting cars for all markets, came in January 1982 when a driver's airbag and seatbelt pre-tensioners

US models had round headlights like the European four-cylinder models. This is a 300CD Turbodiesel coupé.

became an extra-cost option. For 1985, the other US states followed the Californian lead in requiring the turbocharged diesel coupés to have a ceramic particulates filter (usually called a DPF – Diesel Particulates Filter) in the exhaust system. Production of the three coupé models continued until mid-August 1985 when the final car, a 280CE, came off the lines.

Production of C123 models fell just short of 100,000; the figure was actually 99,884. Nearly a third of these had been top-model 280CE types, which indicated quite clearly where the market for Mercedes' medium-sized coupés lay. There had been no convertible variants of the C123 from the factory, but that had not prevented some aftermarket specialists, such as Crayford in Britain, from developing conversions and building them in penny numbers.

MODELS: 230C, 230CE, 280C, 280CE, 300CD, 300CD Turbodiesel.
ENGINES: 2307cc M115 petrol four with 109PS (230C); 2299cc M102 petrol four with 136PS and fuel-injection (230CE); 2746cc M110 DOHC petrol six with 156PS (280C); 2746cc M110 DOHC petrol six with fuel-injection and 177PS, or (from 1978) 185PS (280CE); US models with 142bhp or 137bhp 2998cc (quoted as 3005cc until August 1978) OM617 diesel five with 80PS, or (from September 1979) 88PS (300CD); 2998cc OM617 turbocharged diesel five with 125bhp or 118bhp (300CD Turbodiesel).
GEARBOXES: Four-speed manual standard Five-speed manual optional except on 230C and 280C. Four-speed automatic.

SUSPENSION, STEERING & BRAKES: Front suspension with twin wishbones, coil springs, hydraulic telescopic dampers and anti-roll bar. Rear suspension with semi-trailing arms, coil springs, hydraulic telescopic dampers and anti-roll bar; hydro-pneumatic self-levelling optional on saloons and standard on estates and long-wheelbase models. Recirculating-ball steering, with standard power assistance. Disc brakes on all four wheels, with servo assistance and dual hydraulic circuit; ABS optional from August 1980.
DIMENSIONS: Length: 4640mm. **Width:** 1786mm. **Height:** 1395mm. **Wheelbase:** 2710mm. **Track:** 1488mm (front), 1446mm (rear).
PERFORMANCE & FUEL CONSUMPTION: 230C 106mph, 22mpg, 0-100km/h in 14 sec; 230CE 112mph, 22mpg, 0-100km/h in 12 sec ; 280C manual 118mph, 18mpg, 0-100km/h in 10.5 sec; 280C automatic 118mph, 18mpg, 0-100km/h in 11.5 sec; 280CE manual 124mph, 18mpg, 0-100km/h in 10 sec; 280CE automatic 124mph, 18mpg, 0-100km/h in 11 sec; 300CD manual 92.5mph, 22.5mpg, 0-100km/h in 20 sec; 300CD automatic 92.5mph, 21mpg, 0-100km/h in 21 sec; 300CD Turbodiesel 102.5mph, 21mpg, 0-100km/h in 15 sec.
PRODUCTION TOTALS: 230C: 18,675; 230CE: 29,858; 280C: 3704; 280CE: 32,138; 300CD 7502; 300CD Turbodiesel: 8007.

The C126 coupés, 1979-1991

The C107 SLC coupés were an expedient compromise that was somewhat grudgingly accepted at Stuttgart, but for the next generation of big coupés the decision was made to base them once again on the top-model saloons and to align them more clearly with the flagship S-Class cars. The result was one of the most stunningly attractive cars ever to be produced by Mercedes, and one that was not only a major success when new, but has also gone on to become a coveted classic.

Design of the coupé body was held over until the basic shape of the parent W126 saloons had been established during 1976. The cars were to be based on a short-wheelbase version of the W126 platform –

The big C126 coupés had a very special elegance. This is an early model, with ribbed lower flank panels.

The C126 models had a pillarless design, and many were fitted with the alloy wheel option seen here.

From 1985, the face-lifted cars came with smooth panels on their lower flanks, and the alloy wheels also had a different design.

The top model of the later range came with the 5.6-litre V8 engine and was badged as a 560SEC.

shortened by the same 85mm as the coupé versions of the smaller 123-series cars – but in the end the coupés shared no common exterior panels with the saloons. Designer Bruno Sacco gave them the 'sports' grille of the SLC range rather than the more formal saloon type, and he gave the coupé body more steeply raked front and rear screens than the saloons, plus a long, elegant rear pillar that swept seamlessly into the rear wings. The chosen shape was refined in the wind-tunnel.

The dashboard was more closely related to the saloon type, but had a rev counter in place of the large clock. Velour upholstery was standard, with leather as an option, and there were two individually shaped rear seats instead of a bench. Brand new was a powered retractable arm to present each front seat occupant with a safety belt at a convenient position. Engines were all to be V8s, and there would be no entry-level six-cylinder option this time. ABS was specified as standard because these were flagship models, together with floating-caliper brakes and larger discs on the front wheels.

The new C126 coupés were announced at the Frankfurt show in 1981, two years after the saloons went on sale. There were just two models, a 380SEC and a 500SEC and, as their release coincided with the announcement of Mercedes' Energy Concept initiative, they incorporated all the relevant features of that programme. Alloy wheels were standard for some markets but not for all, and the USA received only the 380SEC, burdened with the same power-sapping emissions control

The SEC models attracted many aftermarket specialists, and this pre-face-lift model was turned into a cabriolet by Vantagefield of London. (Vantagefield)

equipment, rectangular front light units and slightly extended bumpers as the US-model W126 saloons.

Waiting lists built up quickly and dealers were soon quoting delivery delays of 15-18 months. So the 1983 models had no major revisions but only minor changes that included the option of a trip computer. For the USA, the 500SEC now joined the 380SEC.

A mid-life makeover was announced at the same time as that for the saloons, in September 1985. Visual changes were limited to redesigned bumper aprons and smooth-surfaced flank panels, plus new 15-inch wheels with low-profile tyres and a flat-faced alloy wheel option. The 500SEC had several engine improvements and now became the central model of the coupé range, as the 380SEC gave way to a big-bore 420SEC and a more expensive 560SEC with the new 300PS 5.6-litre V8 joined the line-up. All three were available for both Europe and the USA, and all had switchable four-speed automatic gearboxes. European models now came with catalytic converters or were ready to receive them. The KAT models became standard in Germany from September 1986, but production of the others continued until 1989.

Raised compression ratios from September 1987 brought the same power improvements as for the saloons, and from September 1988 the flank panels and aprons were body-coloured. The 1989 and later models had a new style of seat pleating, and could also be had with a passenger's side

airbag, which was made standard in the USA and some other countries. The SEC coupés then remained in production until autumn 1991; assembly of the 500SEC ended in September and the final 420 SEC and 560 SEC types were built a month later. Just over 74,000 of all types had been made.

All the SECs were assembled at the Mercedes plant in Sindelfingen, and there were never any special variants. However, the cars did attract aftermarket specialists who developed bespoke performance and cosmetic upgrades. Cabriolet, Gullwing coupé, and 'wide body' conversions were quite popular in the Middle East, and there were also add-on bodykits in the spirit of the era.

MODELS: 380SEC, 420SEC, 500SEC, 560SEC.
ENGINES: 3818cc (3839cc from 1981) M116 petrol V8 with 204PS (380SEC). 4196cc M116 petrol V8 with 218PS or 231PS from September 1987; 204PS with KAT, or 224PS from September 1987 (420SEC). 4973cc M117 petrol V8 with 231PS, 245PS from September 1985, or 265PS from September 1987; 223PS with KAT, or 252PS from September 1987 (500SEC). 5547cc M117 petrol V8 with 300PS; 279PS with KAT (560SEC).
GEARBOXES: Four-speed automatic.
SUSPENSION, STEERING & BRAKES: Front suspension with wishbones, coil springs with auxiliary rubber springs and anti-roll bar. Rear suspension with semi-trailing arms, coil springs

with auxiliary rubber springs, and anti-roll bar; optional self-levelling strut. Recirculating-ball steering with standard power assistance. Disc brakes all round, ventilated on front wheels and solid on rears; twin hydraulic circuits and vacuum servo assistance; ABS optional to September 1985 and standard afterwards.
DIMENSIONS: Length: 4910mm; 5060mm for US Models. **Width:** 1820mm. **Height:** 1406mm. **Wheelbase:** 2850mm. **Track:** 1545mm (front), 1517mm (rear).
PERFORMANCE & FUEL CONSUMPTION: The spread of figures shown here reflects changes in specification over the years. 380SEC: 130mph, 14mpg, 0-100km/h in 9.5 sec; 420SEC: 136-138mph, 21mpg, 0-100km/h in 8.2-8.3 sec; 500SEC: 140-146mph, 20mpg, 0-100km/h in 7.2-7.8 sec; 560SEC: 141-155mph, 18mpg, 0-100km/h in 6.8-7.6 sec.

PRODUCTION TOTALS: 380SEC: 11,267; 420SEC: 3692; 500SEC: 30,184; 560SEC: 28,929.

The 124 cabriolets and coupés, 1987-1996

Two-door derivatives of the **124** series were in the plan from the beginning, to continue the tradition of pillarless coupés that had begun with the W114 models in 1968. The C124 models were introduced in March 1987, nearly two years after the saloons and estates, and were always built in smaller volumes than their four-door siblings.

The coupés were once again built on a shorter wheelbase than the parent saloons, but their less spacious cabins were balanced by an exquisite appearance clearly derived

The C124 coupés maintained a strong relationship to their parent saloons and were once again pillarless. This is an early example.

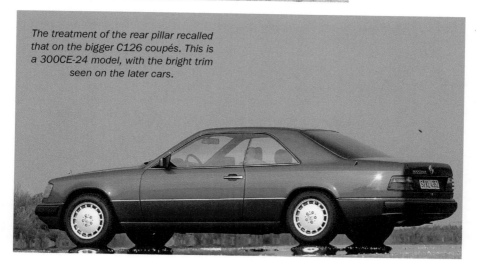

The treatment of the rear pillar recalled that on the bigger C126 coupés. This is a 300CE-24 model, with the bright trim seen on the later cars.

The special light units on coupés for the USA were the same as those on the W124 saloons for that country. This is a 300CE.

two-door range and developed a cabriolet derivative as a second stage. This went on sale in March 1992 after an autumn 1991 announcement, but only a 300CE-24 model was available at this stage. It came as standard with the automatic rollover protection system pioneered on the R129 SL models, and a power-operated soft top was available at extra cost.

from the saloons, while recalling the bigger C126 coupés. From the start, they had plastic protection panels on their lower flanks. Engines, transmissions, suspension, steering and brakes were all shared with the saloons, while the interior mixed 124 saloon elements with the automatic seatbelt arm of the 126 coupés. The first range consisted of a four-cylinder 230CE and a six-cylinder 300CE, with five-speed manual or four-speed automatic gearboxes. Only the 300CE was sold in the USA.

Only minor specification changes were made before the autumn 1989 face-lift, which was shared with the other 124 models. This brought additional exterior brightwork and the Sportline option. There were also two new variants: Italy received a 200CE while a new top model 300CE-24 came with the new four-valve six-cylinder engine. The 24-valve car replaced the 300CE in the USA, where it was nevertheless badged as a plain 300CE.

Mercedes went a step further with this

The next major changes were spread over two years, just as for the other 124 models. In September 1992, the four existing engines gave way to three new ones, all four-valve types. The new models were the four-cylinder 200CE and 220CE, and the six-cylinder 320CE; only the six-cylinder could be had as a cabriolet at this stage. The second set of changes followed a year later, when the rebranding exercise left them as E200, E220 and E230 models, all now available as either coupé or cabriolet. At the same time, E36 AMG models of both were added to the line-up.

Production was brought to an end in March 1996 for the coupés, but there was enough demand for Mercedes to continue building cabriolets until summer 1997. The C124s were the last two-door range to share styling with their

The C124 design adapted extremely well to create an open car. This is an early model, pictured with the top down.

As always, a great deal of care went into the design of the soft top to make it blend well with the lines of the body. This is a 300CE-24 model.

parent saloons, and their successors were created as part of a separate programme from the W210 models that replaced the four-door derivatives of the 124 series.

MODELS: Coupés: 200CE, 220CE, 230CE, 300CE, 300CE-24, 320CE, E200, E220, E320, E36 AMG. **Cabriolets:** 300CE-24, E200, E220, E320, E36 AMG.

ENGINES: 1997cc M102 petrol four with 122PS, or 118PS (KAT) (200CE). 1998cc M111 DOHC petrol four with 136PS (200CE, E200). 2199cc M111 DOHC petrol four with 150PS (220CE), E220. 2299cc M102 petrol four with 136PS or 132PS (KAT) (230CE). 2962cc M103 petrol six with 190PS, or 185PS (KAT) (300CE). 2960cc M104 DOHC petrol six with 220PS (300CE-24). 3199cc M104 DOHC petrol six with 220PS (320CE, E320). 3604cc M104 DOHC petrol six with 272PS (E36 AMG).

GEARBOXES: Five-speed manual. Five-speed close-ratio manual, from 1989. Four-speed automatic.

SUSPENSION, STEERING & BRAKES: Front suspension with MacPherson struts, wishbones, coil springs and anti-roll bar. Rear suspension with five links, coil springs and anti-roll bar; Sportline lowered suspension option from late 1989. Power-assisted recirculating-ball steering. Disc brakes all round, ventilated on some models; dual hydraulic circuit and servo assistance; ABS optional on early 230CE and standard

on 300CE; standard on all models from September 1988.

DIMENSIONS: Length: 4655mm. **Width:** 1740mm. **Height:** 1410mm or (from November 1988) 1395mm. **Wheelbase:** 2715mm. **Track:** 1497mm (front), 1488mm (rear).

PERFORMANCE & FUEL CONSUMPTION: Figures shown are for non-KAT models except where a KAT was standard. KAT versions typically had a top speed around 2mph lower than non-KAT versions and took around 0.2 sec longer to reach 100km/h. Figures shown are for automatic models; manual-gearbox cars typically had a slightly higher top speed. 200CE (M102): 118mph, 30mpg, 0-100km/h in 12.3 sec; 200CE (M111)/E200: 121mph, 33mpg, 0-100km/h in 12 sec; 220CE/ E220: 127mph, 33mpg, 0-100km/h in 10.6 sec; 230CE: 123mph, 30-32mpg, 0-100km/h in 10.4 sec; 300CE: 138mph, 27-28mpg, 0-100km/h in 8.2 sec; 300CE-24: 144mph, 28mpg, 0-100km/h in 7.8 sec; 320CE/E320: 143mph, 26mpg, 0-100km/h in 7.8 sec; E36 AMG: 155mph, 27mpg, 0-100km/h in 7.0 sec.

PRODUCTION TOTALS: 200CE (M102): 5921; 200CE (M111)/E200 coupé: 7848; E200 cabriolet: 6922; 220CE/E220 coupé: 12,337; E220 cabriolet: 8458; 230CE: 33,675; 300CE: 43,486; 300CE-24 coupé: 24,463; 300CE-24 cabriolet: 6343; 320CE/E320 coupé: 13,768 (includes E36 AMG); 320CE/ E320 cabriolet: 12,229 (includes E36 AMG).

The C140 coupés, 1992-1998

The C140 coupés that followed the C126 models were a huge disappointment for Mercedes, and also for their customers. The cars were derived in the usual way from the S-Class saloons and, like the W140 models, were conceived at a time of economic boom but reached the market just as that boom was turning to bust. They never achieved anything like the success of their predecessors.

These coupés were based on a shortened W140 saloon platform, but their sheer bulk meant that only 45mm could be removed to retain good proportions. The addition of an SL-like front end did not make them look any more sporting, and the curious wrapover headlamp units were a miscalculation. *Car* magazine memorably described the C140 as "ugly, thirsty and arrogant" when it was new.

The parent saloons had already gone on sale by the time the C140 was introduced at the Detroit show in January 1992; a European launch at Geneva followed, and then sales began in the summer. As befitted the intended flagship status, only two engines were available, a V8 for the 500SEC and the new M120 V12 for the 600SEC. These names lasted for just one year, and from August 1993 the two models were renamed in accordance with the latest Mercedes policy, becoming S500 and S600 coupés, although the word 'coupé' was never part of their badging.

The range was expanded in April 1994 when a new S420 entry-level model was

The C140 models were undeniably big and bulky, but they also had a certain elegance of their own.

The lines worked very well from the rear, although the dropped window line was questionable.

Not a lot changed on the C140 coupés at the time of the 1994 face-lift; they had already found their audience.

This late-model car shows the CL model name that arrived in 1996, and displays the Parktronic parking radar in its rear bumper.

introduced. A new alloy wheel design arrived at the same time, and self-levelling was made standard on the S600. The range was renamed yet again in June 1996, when the three models became a CL420, CL500 and CL600 respectively. At the same time, Nappa leather upholstery became standard (mainly to meet US tastes) along with Parktronic front and rear parking radar. From January 1997, Brake Assist was also added to the standard specification, but there were no changes of note after that.

Mercedes brought production of the C140 models to a close during 1998, the CL420 ending in August, with the CL500 and CL600 models following in September. Only 26,022 had been made in six years of production, for an annual average of just over 4300 cars. Their C126 predecessors had sold around 74,000 in 10 years for an annual average of 7400. It should therefore be no surprise that the C140s were not mourned by many people.

MODELS: S420 coupé/CL420, 500SEC/S500 coupé/CL500, 600SEC/S600 coupé/CL600.

ENGINES: 4196cc M119 petrol V8 with 279 PS (S420 coupé & CL420). 4973cc M119 petrol V8 with 320 PS (500SEC, S 500 coupé & CL500). 5987cc M120 petrol V12 with 394 PS (600SEC, S600 coupé & CL600).

GEARBOXES: Four-speed automatic (to 1995). Five-speed automatic (from 1995).

SUSPENSION, STEERING & BRAKES: Front suspension with twin wishbones, coil springs, and anti-roll bar. Rear suspension with five links, coil springs, and anti-roll bar. Self-levelling rear suspension optional on all petrol models, and adaptive damping optional with it; hydro-pneumatic suspension optional, then standard on V12 models from April 1994. Recirculating-ball steering with variable ratio and power assistance. Ventilated disc brakes all round, with power assistance and ABS.

DIMENSIONS: Length: 5054mm. **Width:** 1905mm. **Height:** 1455mm. **Wheelbase:** 2945mm. **Track:** 1602mm (front), 1574mm (rear).

PERFORMANCE & FUEL CONSUMPTION: S420, etc: 155mph, 28mpg, 0-100km/h in 8.5 sec; S500, etc: 155mph (limited), 27mpg, 0-100km/h in 7.3 sec; S600, etc: 155mph

(limited), 23mpg, 0-100km/h in 6.6 sec.
PRODUCTION TOTALS: S420, etc: 2496; S500, etc: 14,953; S600, etc: 8573.

The W208 coupés and cabriolets, 1998-2002

Mercedes had made clear in the late 1980s that the coupé and cabriolet derivatives of the 124 series would be the last of their kind based on the medium-sized saloon range. As early as March 1993, its thinking on replacement models was previewed at the Geneva Show by a striking show car – known only as the Mercedes Concept Coupé – that previewed the twin-oval-headlamp styling which would become a Mercedes hallmark a few years later. This was, incidentally, the company's first-ever show car; it was visually very close to the eventual production model, although some of its deliberate show-car features would not reach production.

With the CLK, the mid-range coupés were for the first time based on the compact saloons rather than the medium-sized models.

The upswept rear window tended to make the cars look fatter than they were from some angles. This one is a CLK200.

Although alloy wheels were commonly specified, they were not universal. This CLK230 Kompressor had steel wheels with a bright finish.

There was a certain irony in that the show car had the platform and running-gear of the then-current W124 500E, but of course Mercedes was not yet ready to reveal the intended platform, which would be that of the then-unreleased W202 compact saloons. The real thing would share their wheelbase, their double-wishbone front and multi-link rear suspension, and their power-assisted recirculating-ball steering. It would be known as the CLK model (C-Class, Lightweight, and K for Kurz (meaning short)), and would have the W208 designation.

By the time the production car was previewed at the Detroit show in January 1997, the W210 E-Class models were already on sale, and the new coupé's oval headlights helped to persuade customers that it was a relative of theirs rather than of the smaller C-Class. Unlike the C124 models it replaced, the W208 coupé was not pillarless, but black-out glass did a good job of concealing the upper B-pillar to give the impression that it was. An upswept waistline suggested forward motion, while thick rear pillars hinted at the haunches of an animal ready to pounce.

The cabriolet models lacked the space of the earlier C124 types, but were still an attractive proposition. This one is a 1998 CLK320.

High-performance derivatives were created in response to customer interest, and the bodykit and wheels mark out this cabriolet as a CLK55 AMG model.

Sales began in June 1997 with two trim levels – Sport and Elegance. All cars had a split-folding rear-seat backrest to increase luggage space, and side airbags and seatbelt pre-tensioners were standard for most countries. A foot-operated parking brake was at odds with the car's sporting nature, but there was a long and tempting list of extra-cost options. The choice of three engines created a CLK200, a CLK230 Kompressor, and a CLK320 (with the latest 3.2-litre V6). Specifications and model availability varied from one country to another, but there would never be any diesel CLKs.

The cabriolet models followed a year later, their neat metal tonneau with small speedster-type humps over the hood-well giving a very clean look at the rear. Body reinforcements made them heavier than the coupés, and there were some space compromises in the rear seat area. Both a power-operated soft top and pop-up rear headrests (as pioneered on the R129 SLs) were standard features, and the cabriolets came with the same engines as

The close-fitting cabriolet roof is seen here on a UK-registered CLK230 Kompressor.

the coupés. They were an immediate hit and Mercedes had to increase build volumes to meet demand.

September 1999 brought the expected mid-life face-lift, characterised by body-coloured sills and bumper inserts in place of the earlier black ones, and indicator repeaters on the door mirrors. There were several interior changes as well, and the Sport trim option gave way to an Avantgarde specification. Other new features included electronic safety aids and the standardisation of ESP on all models. The range expanded again, too, to include V8-engined CLK430 coupés and cabriolets, with five-speed automatic gearboxes and stiffer Sport suspension as standard.

The first AMG variant now arrived as a CLK55 AMG, available initially only as a coupé. It was not part of the original range plan, but a one-off AMG safety car used at F1 events led to demand for copies. Distinguishing features included reshaped side skirts, a new front apron with larger air intake slots, and round driving lamps instead of the shaped ones on other CLKs. A cabriolet version followed soon afterwards.

The final major changes came in spring 2000, with some uprated engines. The range now consisted of a 163PS CLK200 Kompressor, a more powerful CLK230 with 197PS, plus the existing CLK320, CLK430 and CLK55 AMG. All the four-cylinder models now gained a six-speed manual gearbox as standard. Just over a year later, the 2002 models took on door mirrors with integral turn signal repeaters, but these would be the last of the first-generation CLKs.

Not to be overlooked, however, is the 1999 CLK GTR, which shared only its instruments, headlamps and grille with the mainstream CLK models. The GTR had started life in 1997 as a pure race car with a carbon-fibre monocoque body and a mid-mounted 6.9-litre V12 engine developed by AMG from the 6-litre type used in the S-Class cars. Race regulations required a homologation run of 25 cars for public sale, and those were built by AMG as two-seat millionaires' playthings.

Production of the standard W208 coupés came to an end in May 2002, and that of the cabriolets continued into 2003, when both were replaced by the new C209 CLK models.

The whole range had been another success for Mercedes, who had sold 278,000 examples in just five years. It reported that some 40% of buyers were new to Mercedes – and that most of those were younger than the marque's traditional buyers. The best seller was the CLK320 coupé, of which 68,778 were built.

MODELS: Coupé and cabriolet: CLK200, CLK 200 Kompressor, CLK 230 Kompressor, CLK320, CLK 430, CLK 55 AMG.

ENGINES: 1998cc M111 petrol four with 136PS (CLK 200). 1998cc M111 supercharged petrol four with 192PS or (from 2000) 163PS. (CLK 200 Kompressor). 2295cc M111 supercharged petrol four with 193PS or (from 2000) 197PS. 3199cc M112 petrol V6 with 218PS (CLK 320). 4266cc M113 petrol V8 279 PS (CLK 430). 5439cc M113 petrol V8 with 347 PS (CLK 55 AMG).

GEARBOXES: Five-speed manual (to May 2000). Six-speed manual with optional Sequentronic shift (from May 2000). Five-speed automatic standard on V6 and V8 models, optional on four-cylinders.

SUSPENSION, STEERING & BRAKES: Front suspension with double wishbones, coil springs, and anti-roll bar. Rear suspension with five links, coil springs, and anti-roll bar. Recirculating-ball steering with power assistance. Disc brakes all round, ventilated at the front; power assistance and ABS.

DIMENSIONS: Length: 4567mm. **Width:** 1722mm. **Height:** 1345mm (coupé); 1380mm (cabriolet). **Wheelbase:** 2690mm. **Track:** 1505mm (front); 1474mm (rear).

PERFORMANCE & FUEL CONSUMPTION: The figures below are for coupé models. Cabriolet models were generally heavier and slightly thirstier.
CLK200 Komp (163PS): 138mph, 28mpg, 0-100km/h in 9.1 sec; CLK230 Komp manual: 145mph, 25mpg, 0-100km/h in 8.4 sec; CLK320: 149mph, 25mpg, 0-100km/h in 7.4 sec; CLK430: 155mph (limited), 23mpg, 0-100km/h in 6.4 sec; CLK55 AMG: 155mph (limited), 21mpg, 0-100km/h in 5.4 sec.

PRODUCTION TOTALS: 233,367 coupés; 44,781 cabriolets.

The C215 coupés, 1998-2006

The big coupés developed from the W220 S-Class saloons were given their own project code of C215, and were more of a standalone creation than was usual. Nevertheless, the platform was that of the W220, shortened by 80mm in the wheelbase, and the body was again a lightweight composite of steel, aluminium, magnesium and plastic.

The twin oval lamps were adopted for the C215 models, together with a sports-type grille.

The C215 coupés were large cars, but careful design made them look smaller than they really were – and much sleeker than the C140s they replaced.

There were no obvious visual links to the W220 models. The front end was totally different, with the four oval light units associated with the E-Class models, and the coupés had their own set of alloy wheel designs. Although they had the expected pillarless hardtop, this had rounded rear pillars rather than the usual raked type. An upward slope to the waistline gave a slight wedge shape and contributed to a low drag coefficient. The interior had four full-size seats with the belts integrated into the front pair, and the driving

The range was revised in 2002, and this publicity picture shows the V12-engined CL600.

The rear end had more of a resemblance to the related W220 saloons than the rest of the car did.

compartment was a more sporty and cockpit-like version of that in the W220.

The C215 models were announced in March 1999 as a V8 CL500 and a V12 CL600, but there were no V8 sales before the autumn and the first V12s came in early 2000. Both were laden with new technology (most of which later found its way to the W220, too), including multiple airbags, Active Body Control, world-first Bi-Xenon high-intensity headlights and hydraulic soft-close doors. The V12s also had a fuel-saving cylinder deactivation system.

From May 2000, 'designo' custom-finish packages became available, offering special interior and exterior colours. Then in September 2000 came the first AMG model: the CL55 AMG. A CL 55 AMG F1 Limited Edition was based on the 2000-season C215 Formula 1 safety car, and was the world's first car with carbon-ceramic brake discs. From September 2001, very limited numbers of a V12 AMG model appeared: the CL63 AMG.

Spring 2002 brought a mid-life face-lift. The front end had a new bumper apron, the door mirrors gained puddle lights, and the rear light lenses changed. All models now had the Pre-Safe electronic pre-crash system and a revised satnav. The CL600 changed to the new Biturbo V12 engine, and the CL55 AMG gained a supercharger (although it never wore Kompressor badges).

The final changes in March 2004 brought the CL65 AMG with the uprated V12 engine shared with the Maybach 57S limousine. Now available as four models – a V8, a V12, and AMG derivatives of each – the C215 remained in production until February 2006. More than two-thirds of the 47,984 cars built were V8-engined CL500 models. The yearly average of nearly 7400 C215s was a major recovery after the poor sales of the C140 predecessor model.

There were of course high-performance derivatives, and this one is a CL65 AMG from October 2004.

MODELS: CL500, CL55 AMG, CL55 AMG 'Kompressor', CL600, CL600 Bi-Turbo, CL63 AMG, CL65 AMG Bi-Turbo.

ENGINES: 4966cc M113 petrol V8 with 306 PS (CL500). 5439cc M113 petrol V8 with 360 PS (CL55 AMG). 5439cc M113 supercharged V8 petrol with 500 PS (CL 55 AMG Kompressor). 5513cc M275 Biturbo petrol V12 with 500 PS (CL 600 Bi-Turbo) 5786cc M137 petrol V12 with 367 PS (CL 600). 5980cc M275 Biturbo petrol V12 with 612PS (CL65 AMG). 6258cc M137 petrol V12 with 444 PS (CL63 AMG).

GEARBOXES: Five-speed automatic. Seven-speed automatic

SUSPENSION, STEERING & BRAKES: Front suspension with four links, hydro-pneumatic height-adjustment, air-operated dampers and anti-roll bar. Rear suspension with five links, hydro-pneumatic height-adjustment, air-operated dampers and anti-roll bar. Rack-and-pinion steering with power assistance.

Disc brakes all round, ventilated front and rear; power assistance and ABS.

DIMENSIONS: Length: 4993mm. **Width:** 1857mm. **Height:** 1398mm. **Wheelbase:** 2885mm. **Track:** 1577mm (front), 1578mm (rear).

PERFORMANCE & FUEL CONSUMPTION: CL500: 155mph (limited), 21mpg, 0-100km/h in 6.5sec. CL 55 AMG: 155mph (limited), 21mpg, 0-100km/h in 6.0sec. CL 55 AMG 'Kompressor': 155mph (limited), 20mpg, 0-100km/h in 4.8sec. CL 600 (M137): 155mph (limited), 21mpg, 0-100km/h in 6.3sec. CL 600 (M275): 155mph (limited), 21mpg, 0-100km/h in 4.8sec. CL63 AMG: 155mph (limited), 20mpg, 0-100km/h in 5.5sec. CL65 AMG: 155mph (limited), 19mpg, 0-100km/h in 4.4 sec.

PRODUCTION TOTALS: CL 500: 32,224; CL 600 (M137): 6348; CL 600 (M275): 2255; CL 55 AMG: 2217; CL 55 AMG Komp: 4163; CL 63 AMG: 26; CL 65 AMG: 777.

The W168 A-class, 1997-2004

The oil crises of the 1970s set Mercedes on the path of designing a small car, which eventually came to fruition as the W168 A-Class. Early difficulties with crashworthiness in prototypes with a traditional front-engined layout led to a series of radical solutions, among which was a unique 'sandwich' construction with the cabin floor set above the underside of the monocoque, leaving a space between the two into which the engine would be pushed in the case of a frontal impact.

The radical design of the A Class resulted in a shape unlike that of any previous Mercedes. This early model is probably an A140.

To save space, the W168 was designed with transverse engines and front-wheel drive; these and other ingenious solutions led to the design of a short but tall one-box body shape unlike that of any previous Mercedes, with a new range of compact petrol and diesel engines. More clever design ensured that the passenger cabin was remarkably large, with flexible seating as well.

The A-Class was announced at the Frankfurt show in autumn 1997 as a four-model range. The petrol models were the A140 and A160, while A160 CDI and A170 CDI were turbocharged and intercooled diesels. Three trim levels were available: Classic, Elegance and Avantgarde, but only manual gearboxes were available at this stage.

The tall, narrow body could look quite ungainly from some angles, but many buyers found the shape appealing. This is a 2001 standard-wheelbase model.

In Sweden, early production examples failed the so-called 'elk test' of a double-swerve avoidance manoeuvre. Mercedes halted sales, rapidly redeveloped the suspension and added ESP stability control as standard, and put the revised models into production in February 1998. They also modified large numbers of earlier production models to the new standard, and from then on the A-Class sold strongly.

The range was expanded in July 1998 with an automatic gearbox option, then again in autumn 1999 with a 'sports' gearbox option and a long-stroke A190 with a sporty bodykit. These 2000-model revisions were accompanied by trim and equipment changes across the range. From June 2000 the automatic A140 changed to a detuned 1.6-litre engine in order to meet new emissions regulations.

The mid-life face-lift was introduced in

The rear view was no more conventional than the front, and without the three-pointed star it would have been difficult to identify the manufacturer.

A bodykit helped the A190 model to stand out from the others.

From the side, the bigger rear door of the long-wheelbase models arguably produced a better-balanced result.

February 2001. Visual changes were minor, affecting the grille, headlights, bumpers and alloy wheel options. More important was the introduction of long-wheelbase models that increased overall interior space by 11%; these had the existing engines but were identified by an L in their model names. Meanwhile, both diesel engines received power increases. The facia was reshaped, more airbags could be had at extra cost, and suspension changes improved both ride and handling.

In early 2002 the A210 Evolution models added more performance to the range with a long-stroke version of the A190 engine, an AMG-designed bodykit and stiffer suspension. Real AMG models never reached production, although two were designed – one with a 3.2-litre M112 V6 engine, and the other with twin engines, one in the front and one at the rear.

The W168 also had a spin-off in the 414-series Vaneo light commercial range, which met with disappointing sales. The cars were built at Mercedes' Rastatt plant in Germany, but there was also CKD assembly in Brazil and Thailand.

Production in Germany ended in 2004 after around 1.1 million A-Class models had been made. The most popular model was the A170 CDI, and the long-wheelbase models accounted for more than 40% of cars built.

Top of the range by the time production ended was the 140PS A210 Evolution, which could reach 60mph from rest in under 8 seconds.

Numerically, the model was a success but the huge initial development costs and the rework costs early in its life ensured that Mercedes lost money on every one.

MODELS: A140, A140L, A160, A160CDI, A160L, A170CDI, A190, A190L, A210 Evolution, A210 Evolution (LWB).
ENGINES: 1397cc M166 petrol four with 82PS (A140 & A140L). 1598cc M166 petrol four with 82PS (A140 automatic & A140L automatic). 1598cc M166 petrol four with 102PS (A160 & A160L). 1689cc OM668 diesel four with 60PS, or (from 2001) 75PS

(A160 CDI). 1689cc 0M668 diesel four with 90PS, or (from 2001) 95PS (A170 CDI & A170CDI L). 1898cc M166 petrol four with 125PS (A190 & A190L). 2084cc M166 petrol four with 140PS (A210 Evolution & A210 Evolution LWB).

GEARBOXES: Five-speed manual. Five-speed manual with Automatic Clutch System. Five-speed automatic from mid-1998.

SUSPENSION, STEERING & BRAKES: Front suspension with wishbones, McPherson struts, and anti-roll bar. Rear suspension with trailing arms, coil springs, and anti-roll bar. Rack-and-pinion steering with electric power assistance. Disc front brakes (ventilated on LWB and some other models) and drum rear brakes (solid rear discs on some later models), with power assistance and ABS.

DIMENSIONS: Length: 3575mm or (from 2001) 3606mm; 3776mm for LWB models. **Width:** 1719mm. **Height:** 1575-1589mm. **Wheelbase:** 2423mm or 2593mm (LWB). **Track:** 1523mm (front), 1472mm (rear).

PERFORMANCE & FUEL CONSUMPTION: A140: 105mph, 40mpg, 0-100km/h in 12.9 sec; A140 auto: 103mph, 37mpg, 0-100km/h in 14.6 sec; A160: 113mph, 39mpg, 0-100km/h in 10.8 sec; A160 CDI: 95mph, 59mpg, 0-100km/h in 17.6 sec; A170 CDI (90 PS): 108mph, 58mpg, 0-100km/h in 12.5 sec; (95 PS): 112mph, 58mpg, 0-100km/h in 12 sec; A170 CDI L: 111mph, 58mpg, 0-100km/h in 12.1 sec; A190: 123mph, 36mpg, 0-100km/h in 8.8 sec; A210 Evo: 126mph, 36mpg, 0-100km/h in 8.2 sec; A210 Evo auto: 123mph, 34mpg, 0-100km/h in 9.0 sec.

PRODUCTION TOTALS: 1,100,000 approx.

The W163 ML Class, 1998-2005

The W163 ML Class was yet another indication that the Mercedes marque was expanding its horizons during the 1990s, this time to include the rapidly-growing market for family-oriented SUVs (Sport Utility Vehicles). After a plan to build a vehicle jointly with Mitsubishi was abandoned, the company decided not only to design its own but also to establish a new factory to build it in the USA, where the biggest sales of the SUV could be expected. The site selected was in Vance, Alabama.

The SUV development programme took the W163 designation and started in 1993. The production model then went on sale in 1998, initially in the USA but also in Europe that autumn. Originally intended to be called an M-Class, it became the ML-Class when BMW objected that some model-names would clash with their M-badged models from the Motorsport division.

The W163 was deliberately styled with more rounded lines than most contemporary rivals to give a less rugged look. A dual-range transfer box gave off-road ability, but the 4x4 system was primarily used to improve traction on the road. Structurally, there was a separate chassis but the stiff bodyshell contributed 70% of overall torsional rigidity.

Engines were drawn from those already in production for Mercedes cars, and the choice catered for all markets. Outside the USA, there were four-cylinder petrol (ML230) and 2.7-litre diesel (ML270 CDI) models, while a 3.2-litre petrol V6 (ML320) and 4.3-litre petrol V8

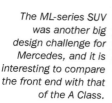

The ML-series SUV was another big design challenge for Mercedes, and it is interesting to compare the front end with that of the A Class.

The rear end treatment was controversial at first, but the thick rearmost pillar introduced a new design language to the SUV market.

(ML430) provided models for the USA and for the top end of the European market. All came with five-speed automatic gearboxes, although a manual was available for the ML230.

Early build quality was notoriously variable, and it took a long time for Mercedes to tackle the issues successfully; meanwhile the ML-Class came bottom of a JD Power quality survey. Despite such problems, the model sold very well, and Mercedes pressed on with its planned next stages. A better-quality interior was central to the changes for the 2000 model-year, but it was accompanied by a new high-performance model: the 146mph ML55 AMG, which came with some cosmetic body modifications and special wheels.

The usual Mercedes mid-life face-lift came in late 2001 for the 2002 models, and the manufacturer claimed that it incorporated more than 1100 new or modified parts. Visually, the main changes were a restyled front apron that incorporated driving lamps, turn signals in the door mirror bodies, and redesigned bumper assemblies in the body colour instead of the earlier matt grey type.

There were also changes in the model line-up. Some markets received a new ML400 CDI model as a top-of-the-range diesel with an automatic gearbox as standard. The existing ML430 gave way to an ML500, and further changes in 2002 brought an ML350 in place

There were few design changes over the years, and this ML400 CDI did not look very different from the first models.

The ML Class brought a more car-like appearance to a market accustomed to truck-like 4x4s. This 2001 ML400 CDI makes the point.

A bodykit of wider wheelarches was the most obvious distinguishing feature of the high-performance ML55 AMG model. (Spanish Coches, CC by SA 2.0)

of the ML320, although the two co-existed for a time in some markets.

The six-model range of ML 230, ML270 CDI, ML350, ML400 CDI, ML500 and ML55 AMG saw the range to a close in 2005, when the W163 was replaced across the board by a second-generation ML-Class model. No overall production figures have been released but the W163 had sold in satisfyingly large volumes worldwide, and had established the Mercedes-Benz marque as a serious player in the SUV market. Outside the USA, the best seller had been the smaller diesel-engined model, the ML270 CDI.

MODELS: ML230, ML270 CDI, ML320, ML350, ML400 CDI, ML430, ML500, ML55 AMG.

ENGINES: 2295cc M111 petrol four with 150 PS (ML230). 2685cc OM612 diesel five with 163 PS (ML270 CDI). 3199cc M112 petrol V6 with 218 PS (ML320). 3724cc M112 petrol V6 with 235 PS (ML350). 3996cc OM628 diesel V8 with 250 PS (ML400 CDI). 4266cc M113 petrol V8 with 272 PS (ML430). 4966cc M113 petrol V8 with 292 PS (ML500). 5439cc M113 petrol V8 with 347 PS (ML55 AMG).

GEARBOXES: Five-speed manual (ML230 only). Six-speed manual. Five-speed automatic.

SUSPENSION, STEERING & BRAKES: Front suspension with double wishbones, torsion bars and anti-roll bar. Rear suspension with double wishbones, coil springs and anti-roll bar. Rack-and-pinion steering with power assistance. Disc brakes all round, ventilated at the front; power assistance and ABS.

DIMENSIONS: Length: 4587mm or (from 2001) 4638mm; 4638mm or (from 2001) 4635mm (ML55 AMG). **Width:** 1840mm. **Height:** 1804-1820mm. **Wheelbase:** 2820mm. **Track:** 1555mm (front and rear).

PERFORMANCE & FUEL CONSUMPTION: ML270 CDI: 114mph, 30mpg, 0-100km/h in 11.6 sec; ML320: 121mph, 20mpg, 0-100km/h in 9.5 sec; ML350: 127mph, 22mpg, 0-100km/h in 9.1 sec; ML430: 130mph, 20mpg, 0-100km/h in 7.9 sec; ML500: 140mph, 19mpg, 0-100km/h in 7.7 sec; ML55 AMG: 146mph, 19mpg, 0-100km/h in 6.0 sec.

PRODUCTION TOTALS: ML320: 282,614. Overall total not available.

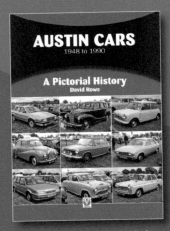

ISBN: 978-1-787112-19-3
Paperback • 21x14.8cm
• 112 pages • 275 colour and
b&w pictures

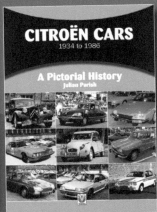

ISBN: 978-1-787116-36-8
Paperback • 21x14.8cm
• 152 pages • 350 pictures

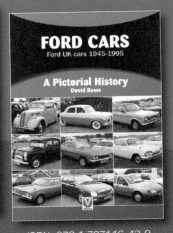

ISBN: 978-1-787116-42-9
Paperback • 21x14.8cm
• 160 pages • 330 pictures

A Pictorial History – the series

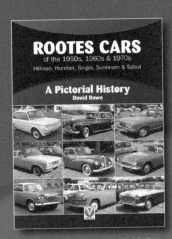

ISBN: 978-1-787114-43-2
Paperback • 21x14.8cm
• 168 pages • 1083 colour and
b&w pictures

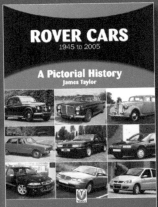

ISBN: 978-1-787116-09-2
Paperback • 21x14.8cm
• 80 pages • 300 pictures

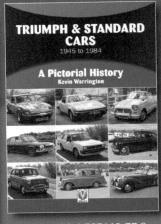

ISBN: 978-1-787110-77-9
Paperback • 21x14.8cm
• 96 pages • 244 colour
pictures

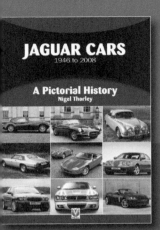

JAGUAR CARS
1946 to 2008

A Pictorial History
Nigel Thorley

ISBN: 978-1-787117-76-1
Paperback • 21x14.8cm
• 160 pages • 387 colour and
b&w pictures

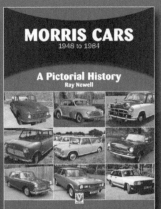

MORRIS CARS
1948 to 1984

A Pictorial History
Ray Newell

ISBN: 978-1-787110-55-7
Paperback • 21x14.8cm
• 144 pages • 425 colour
pictures

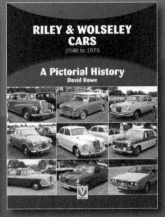

**RILEY & WOLSELEY
CARS**
1948 to 1975

A Pictorial History
David Rowe

ISBN: 978-1-787117-91-4
Paperback • 21x14.8cm
• 104 pages • 352 colour and
b&w pictures

These handy reference books cover all the key models, providing an overview of history
and car design, detailed technical specifications and production data, all illustrated with
hundreds of colour photographs and informative diagrams.

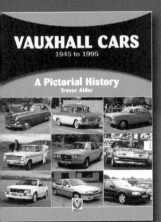

VAUXHALL CARS
1945 to 1995

A Pictorial History
Trevor Alder

ISBN: 978-1-787115-93-4
Paperback • 21x14.8cm
• 160 pages • 339 pictures

VOLVO CARS
1945-1995

A Pictorial History
Trevor Alder

ISBN: 978-1-845846-13-8
Paperback • 21x14.8cm
• 112 pages • 216 pictures

Each book is a valuable
resource for enthusiasts,
and the series as a
whole provides a vast
pool of knowledge for
any automotive library.

For more information, or to order, go to
www.veloce.co.uk

The Essential Buyer's Guide series

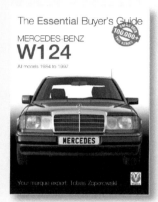

Having one of these books in your pocket is just like having a real marque expert by your side. Benefit from the authors' years of Mercedes-Benz ownership, learn how to spot a bad car quickly, and how to assess a promising car like a professional. Get the right car at the right price!

Paperback • 19.5x13.9cm • 64-96 pages • circa 100 pictures

To see the full range of Essential Buyer's Guides, visit our website at www.veloce.co.uk • email: info@veloce.co.uk

INDEX

NOTE: Mercedes-Benz allocates a three-digit code number to its car programmes. This code was always prefixed by the letter W (Wagen, or car), but in more recent times different letters have been used for the variants of a design. For instance, A = cabriolet, C = coupé, and R = roadster. The index that follows is based on the numerical order, so that W100 comes before R107. Within types, A124 precedes C124, and so on.

Type	Model	Years	Pages
W100	600 limousine	1964-1981	31-34
W105	Ponton saloon	1956-1959	9-12
C107	S-Class coupé	1972-1981	85-87
R107	SL roadster	1971-1989	65-68
W108	Saloon	1965-1971	34-37
W109	Saloon	1965-1971	34-37
W110	Fintail saloon	1961-1968	12-15
W111	Cabriolet	1961-1971	80-82
	Coupé	1961-1971	80-82
	Fintail saloon	1959-1968	12-15
W112	Cabriolet	1961-1971	80-82
	Coupé	1961-1971	80-82
	Fintail saloon	1961-1968	12-15
W113	Pagoda SL	1963-1971	62-65
W114	Stroke 8 coupé	1969-1976	82-85
	Stroke 8 saloon	1968-1976	15-18
W115	Stroke 8 saloon	1968-1976	15-18
W116	S-Class	1972-1980	37-39
W120	Ponton saloon	1953-1962	9-12
W121	Saloon	1956-1962	9-12
	SL roadster	1955-1962	60-62
C123	Coupé	1977-1985	88-90
W123	Saloon	1976-1985	18-21
	Estate	1978-1985	18-21
A124	Cabriolet	1992-1996	94, 95
C124	Coupé	1987-1996	93-95
W124	Estate	1984-1996	21-25
	Saloon	1984-1996	21-25
C126	S-Class coupé	1979-1991	90-93
W126	S-Class	1979-1992	40-42
R129	SL roadster	1989-2001	69-71
W136	170 saloon	1947-1955	6, 7
	170 cabriolet	1949-1951	75, 76
C140	S-Class coupé	1992-1998	96, 97

Type	Model	Years	Pages
W140	S-Class	1991-1998	42-45
W163	ML-Class SUV	1998-2005	105-107
W168	A-Class	1997-2004	103-105
R170	SLK roadster	1996-2004	71-74
W180	Ponton cabriolet	1956-1960	78-80
	Ponton coupé	1956-1960	78-80
	Ponton saloon	1954-1962	9-12
W186	300 limousine	1951-1962	29-31
W187	220 saloon	1951-1954	7-9
	Cabriolet	1951-1955	76, 77
	Coupé	1951-1955	76, 77
W188	300S cabriolet	1951-1958	77, 78
	300S coupé	1951-1958	77, 78
	300S roadster	1951-1958	77, 78
W191	Saloons	1952-1953	7-9
W198	Gullwing coupé	1954-1957	57-59
	Roadster	1957-1963	59
W201	190 saloon	1982-1993	49-53
W202	C-Class estate	1993-2001	53-56
	C-Class saloon	1993-2001	53-56
W208	CLK cabriolet	1999-2002	99, 100
	CLK coupé	1998-2002	97-100
W210	E-Class estate	1995-2003	26-28
	E-Class saloon	1995-2003	26-28
C215	S-Class coupé	1998-2006	100-102
W220	S-Class	1998-2005	45-48